Crystal
Reiki Healing

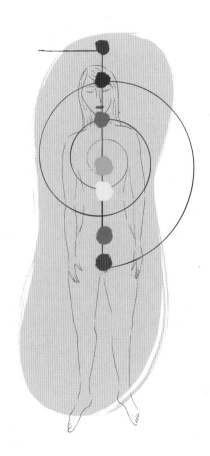

Crystal Reiki Healing

THE POWERHOUSE THERAPY FOR MIND, BODY, AND SPIRIT

PHILIP PERMUTT

CICO BOOKS

LONDON NEW YORK

Published in 2020 by CICO Books
An imprint of Ryland Peters & Small Ltd
20–21 Jockey's Fields   341 E 116th St
London WC1R 4BW   New York, NY 10029

www.rylandpeters.com

10 9 8 7 6 5

A CIP catalog record for this book is available from the Library of
Congress and the British Library.

ISBN: 978 1 78249 857 5

Printed in China

Editor: Carmel Edmonds
Designers: Eliana Holder and Maria Georgiou
Photographers: Roy Palmer and Geoff Dann
Artworks: Trina Dalziel

Commissioning editor: Kristine Pidkameny
In-house editor: Dawn Bates
Art director: Sally Powell
Production controller: David Hearn
Publishing manager: Penny Craig
Publisher: Cindy Richards

SAFETY NOTE
Please note that while the descriptions of the properties of some
crystals refer to healing benefits, they are not intended to replace
diagnosis of illness or ailments, or healing or medicine. Always consult
your doctor or other health professionals in the case of illness.

Contents

Introduction

Once upon a time, in a blue space filled with glittering crystals, the violet energy ray of Reiki found a home… My first crystal shop was painted a medium-light shade of cyan—Pantone 305. It was in that blue space filled with glittering crystals that crystals and Reiki came together for me. I was already teaching crystal healing in the early 1990s when I came across a "new" healing modality called Reiki.

Reiki is a natural healing energy that flows through everyone, although its power can be amplified by becoming attuned to Reiki (see page 14) and learning techniques, such as those given in this book. Crystal healing is amazing, sensational, and can help almost any condition there is. Crystals have an innate energy of their own. They bring everything to balance and speed the body's natural healing ability. You don't have to do anything to get a crystal to work other than place it in your vicinity. However, if you do add your intent, your natural healing thoughts, and your energy, your crystals will work better because they'll pick up your intention and magnify it manyfold. And if Reiki is the energy that is flowing through you, then your crystals will collect the Reiki, multiply its effect, and focus its objective.

Given my background as a scientist, I have a tendency to make notes and record results, which allows me to formalize healing processes, exactly as I have been doing with crystal healing for many years. Crystal Reiki came into being as a result of my enthusiasm and love for both healing energies, and I originally worked on it with my first wife, before going our separate ways. It is a natural progression, combining ancient techniques from these two healing systems into one easily accessible healing modality. The evidence shows us that crystal healing stretches back to the dawn of mankind and although Reiki as brought to us by Usui Sensei (see page 16) is a 20th-century technique, its methods are firmly rooted in antiquity.

Crystal Reiki is a synthesis of universal life force energy, which is what Reiki means and is, and the healing power of the Stone People (another name for crystals). Practicing this healing system at the simplest level can mean holding a crystal and charging it up with Reiki to carry with you during the day or even to give to someone else to help them through a troubling time. Taking the practice further can involve applying intricate and powerful Crystal Reiki Healing grids on the body to treat yourself and others, and even sending healing energy to those far away. Crystal Reiki offers a path to self-development, too: as you practice it and, if you choose, progress through the levels of Reiki attunement, you will gain inner power, a deeper knowledge of yourself, and much more.

Today there are many varieties of Reiki. Throughout this book, all references are to the traditional Usui Reiki system and Tibetan Usui Reiki. Where any of my personal practice differs, I'll try to point this out. However, you can add crystals to whichever system of Reiki you practice, and they will have the same effect of enhancing the healing effects.

Although I may not have been the first person to put crystals and Reiki together, and I will not be the last, the Crystal Reiki Healing system that I present here gives you a set of standard, straightforward techniques that you can follow and practice.

The healing properties of crystals enhance and focus Reiki. Reiki amplifies the effect of healing crystals. They form a beautiful circle. In applying Crystal Reiki in our daily lives, we are limited only by our imagination.

I hope that the Stone People will make your Reiki journey sparkle as they do mine.

chapter 1

combining crystals
AND Reiki

Crystals are the stepping-stones of the soul. Reiki is the violet energy ray that carries our spirit. When they are combined, Crystal Reiki is like hitting the healing overdrive switch! In this chapter, learn more about the background and power of crystals and Reiki, and how the two healing systems can be brought together.

what are crystals?

Crystals are natural living, growing entities. They grow by absorbing molecules from their chaotic environment and layering these molecules in perfectly ordered regular patterns. They bring their surroundings into balance, and they continue to do this energetically in whichever situation they are placed. (Whenever I use the term crystal throughout this book, unless it is to a specific type of crystal such as a quartz crystal or an amethyst crystal, I'm referring to the whole mineral kingdom—crystals, rocks, stones, a pebble on the beach…)

Our auras—the energy fields that surround our bodies—are very sensitive. We often ignore them because that is what we have usually been trained to do by the society we live in. From when we are young, we are told that you can't feel this, see that, or hear whatever. But we do sense energy—we feel it, we see it, and we hear answers to our questions, if we touch, look, and listen with our hearts. We also smell and taste on many levels too. Have you ever tried smelling or listening to a crystal? Or touching a quartz crystal to the tip of your tongue? Try the following exercise and be amazed at how much your senses pick up!

TUNING INTO A CRYSTAL

You will need a hand-sized, natural quartz crystal point for this exercise. Cleanse it before you start (see page 49).

1. Look at the crystal and really explore it with your eyes for a few minutes. Notice its shape and how the light reflects, refracts, and mingles with the crystalline structure. Be aware of the colors within and on the crystal's surface. Register its details in your mind so you could recognize it in a crowd: every crystal is an individual and looks different. Can you see anything around the outside of the crystal?

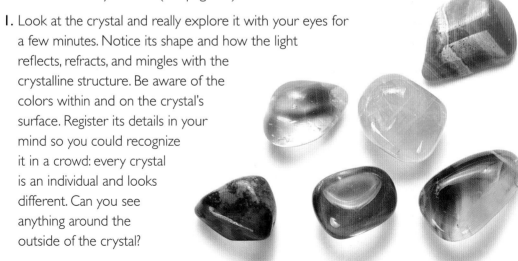

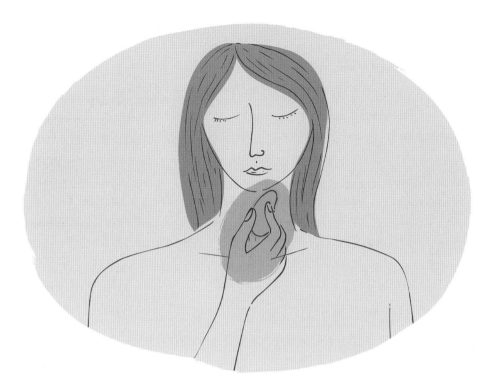

Maybe a subtle haze? If you can, this is the crystal's energy field; the crystal's aura, if you like.

2. Now close your eyes and do the same thing with your fingers. Explore the crystal. *Look* at it with your fingertips. Be aware of how it feels; the flat bits and sharp edges, rough areas and smooth sections. Be aware of its point, the crystal's termination. How does it feel, both physically and emotionally? Again, every crystal feels different. Take a few minutes doing this and allow yourself to be aware of any sensations or emotions you might be feeling in your body.

3. Place your crystal on a table, hold your hands a couple of inches (5 cm) either side of the crystal, and notice the energy you sense. Be patient—this may take a few minutes.

4. Hold the crystal to your ear, as if you were holding a seashell. Listen. What do you hear? Most people can hear a sound like that which you hear when you hold a seashell to your ear. In fact, this is the sound of the crystal vibrating. It isn't quite the same as the sound of a seashell because of the process that creates the sound. With a seashell, the air rushes into and then out from the spiral inside the shell. This creates an indirect noise that sounds like being by the seashore. With your crystal, you are hearing

the actual physical vibration from within the crystal. Different varieties of crystal will vibrate at different speeds, creating and sending higher and lower frequencies to your ear.

5. Smell the crystal. Hold it close to your nose and take a deep breath in. What does it smell like? It might surprise you to know that different types of crystals have subtle, diverse aromas.

6. As long as it is safe to, try tasting the crystal by touching it to the tip of your tongue. Quartz often tastes like fresh mountain air, or slightly lemony. Other crystals create different tastes—for example, amethyst often tastes metallic. These flavors are quite subtle, but once you notice them, they become easier to detect on different crystals.

HOW DO CRYSTALS WORK?

Through interacting with your energy system, your aura, and your chakras (energy hot spots in the body—see page 18), crystals bring balance to the cells in your body, your emotions, your mind, your thoughts, and your senses. They help to relieve stress and bring you back to a place of stability and happiness. Although they act instantly, and many people sense this, it is the longer-term subtle changes that build together to bring life-changing healing effects.

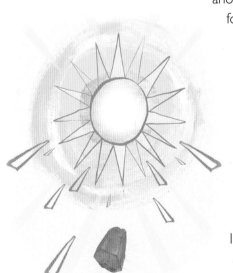

Crystals have electric potential and electric charges. They can store and focus energy, transform it from one type of energy to another, transmute negative energies, and stimulate positive forces. Crystals are found throughout technology: they power your 21st-century lifestyle. Without them you would have no dishwasher, washing machine, tumble dryer, microwave oven, programmable kitchen oven, refrigerator, freezer, music system, DVD player, cell (mobile) phone, or computer. In fact, the laptop that I'm writing this book on wouldn't exist and I'd be writing this manuscript on parchment, using ink made from minerals such as graphite or lapis lazuli, or stone tablets—both of which would still involve the help of our crystal friends! Sometimes people ask me if I believe crystals work… when I receive this question

through my website, by email, or through social media, I always smile at the thought that without our crystal allies they couldn't have even sent the question!

Crystals work by bringing the energies in the world around them into balance. When you are part of that world—that is if you are working with crystals, holding them, wearing them, or even just have them around your home or workplace—they will help to bring your energies into balance, effecting healing. Different varieties of crystals affect different parts of the physical and spiritual bodies, including functions, thoughts, and emotions or feelings. Crystals can help speed healing in many—or all—circumstances. Healing is about change; change from an unhealthy state to a stable healthy position. It is about improving your physical and mental health, your emotional well-being, and your spiritual advancement. Crystals love doing all these things and more.

Phrases such as "we are beings of light," "we come from the light," or "we go back to the light" are common in many religions and spiritual traditions worldwide, and quantum physics has shown this to be the case—we are, in fact, made of photon light and when we die, we do literally go back to the light. Given that quartz crystal focuses light and recent research has shown that light affects how we feel, it is not unreasonable to postulate that as we focus light through a quartz crystal to the area in need of healing that we feel better and healing takes place.

what is Reiki?

Reiki is an amazingly simple but powerful form of spiritual healing practice in which the practitioner channels Reiki (universal life force energy), which is in and around every living being. Using healing and meditation techniques, Reiki healers learn how to focus this energy so that it flows into the recipient. It is said that Reiki has an intelligence of its own and knows where it is required and therein lies its power.

Reiki is for everyone, because everyone has Reiki—it is a completely natural energy. Think of when a child falls and scrapes their knee: their parent places a hand on the knee for a few seconds, and the pain disappears—this is natural Reiki healing energy.

THE THREE LEVELS OF REIKI ATTUNEMENT

Because Reiki is within everyone, everyone can learn how to harness its healing power. However, there is a simple, but deep, experiential process called Reiki attunement, which is performed by a Reiki Master (see below) and connects the student to Reiki. Although there are many styles of attunement in the West, it is customary for the student to be seated, perhaps with symbols beneath them that can be drawn or created with crystals. The Reiki Master channels Reiki and symbols (see page 22) in a precise way to activate or enhance the flow of Reiki through the student, depending on the level the student is being attuned to (see right). The Reiki Master will also teach the student how to channel the energy.

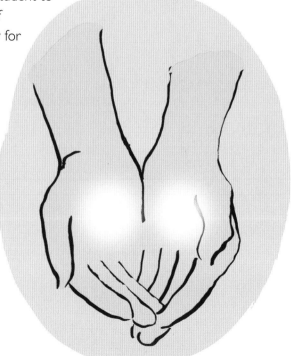

THREE LEVELS

Reiki is usually taught in three levels.

- **Level 1** is called Shoden, meaning beginner teachings: this involves four attunements over a two-day workshop and is about the basics of self-treatment and treating others, and bringing Reiki into everyday life.

- **Level 2** is called Okuden, meaning hidden or inner teachings: this involves two attunements over a two-day workshop, and you learn about more complex treatments, as well as how to use the Reiki symbols (see page 22).

- **Level 3** is called Shinipden, the Reiki Master Teacher level, meaning mystery teachings: this involves one attunement, and, as well as building on the previous levels, it shows how to teach Reiki to others and explores the self-development that Reiki can offer.

The benefit of attunement is that it improves the energy flow. I tell my students to imagine that they are a tube of bamboo. Level 1 attunement knocks out the bits in the middle of the tube, allowing energy to flow through. Level 2 attunement acts like sandpaper, smoothing the inside of the stick for ever better flow. Level 3 attunement smooths the inner channel of the bamboo to a mirror-polished finish—energy can now speed through you.

Once you are attuned to Reiki you always have it literally in the palms of your hands. You can't wear it out and you can't lose it, no matter how little you may use it or even if you forget what you've learned. After attunement, the universal healing energy is always flowing within you. If you touch someone with the intent to heal, or direct your healing Reiki energy, or even just think healing thoughts, you have the potential to facilitate a transformation.

Although anyone can follow the system of Crystal Reiki Healing and you can use the techniques in this book without attunement, visiting a Reiki Master to become attuned to Reiki, at any level, will allow you to discover the full benefits of the Crystal Reiki Healing system. You should not work professionally treating others with Crystal Reiki without completing either Level 1 or a Crystal Reiki course.

REIKI HISTORY AND ORIGINS

The origins of Reiki can be seen to stem from several sources, including Buddhism, Taoism, Chinese and Japanese Shamanism, and several similar Japanese traditions, such as Shinto and Johrei (although the latter might have descended from Reiki). However, the practice of Reiki as we know it was founded in Japan by Mikao Usui (1865–1926), who was also known as Doctor Usui or Usui Sensei (*Sensei* is an honorary title similar to Master). He discovered Reiki in March 1922 during a mystical experience while on a spiritual retreat on Mount Kurama. The word Reiki is formed from the Japanese words *rei* meaning "universal" and *ki* meaning "life force energy."

During his lifetime, Usui Sensei taught about 2,000 Reiki students his way of healing in Japan, including about 16 Reiki Masters who continued his legacy after his death in 1926. The Reiki Master Hawayo Hiromi Takata, who was based in Hawaii, helped introduce Reiki to the West in the 1930s. Because of anti-Japanese feeling in the United States at the time, much of Usui Sensei's story was Americanized, leaving a path of confusion for many. However, we now know that he was a real person who did amazing healing things and who was officially honored by the Japanese government for his services.

REIKI IDEALS

The secret art of inviting happiness
The miraculous medicine of all diseases
Just for today, do not be angry
Do not worry and be filled with gratitude
Devote yourself to your work and
be kind to people
Every morning and every evening join
your hands in prayer,
Pray these words to your heart,
and chant these words with your mouth
Usui Reiki Treatment for the
improvement of body and mind.

The Founder, Usui Mikao (Sensei)

THE BENEFITS OF REIKI

Reiki can help to alleviate many physical problems. In some cases, symptoms completely disappear. Reiki has an amazing ability to both relax and energize you at the same time. It brings stillness to your mind and washes away your worries. But it is when you add Reiki to your individual spiritual journey, your unique path through life, that the true secret is discovered. Usui Sensei described this as "the secret art of happiness," and this is perhaps the greatest benefit of Reiki.

combining crystals and Reiki through the chakras

Crystals are extremely transformative and are especially receptive to Reiki. They love it. Crystals hold Reiki and enhance it, magnifying its effects and generously passing them on. You could say the crystal/Reiki partnership is a match made in heaven—truly blessed. Crystals can focus, store, transmit, and transmute Reiki for beneficial healing and energizing results, and, as a generalization, both crystal energy and Reiki work best when focused through the chakras.

The human energy system is comprised of lines of energy running through the body known as meridians or nadis. These carry ki (also known as chi or prana) through the human (and animal) form and create energy hot spots in the body called chakras. "Chakra" is a Sanskrit word meaning "wheel." Many people believe this is because of the common depiction of chakras as circles on the body, but it is more likely associated with the motion of wheels carrying energy like a water wheel which amplifies its power as it goes. Water is often used symbolically to represent energy. There are many yogic systems that depict the chakras in any number from three to twenty-one, but the most common system used in the West has seven major chakras (see opposite) and many minor chakras, including in the palms of the hands and soles of the feet.

Because these areas have more energy than other parts, chakras are the easiest place for your body to exchange energy with the outside world and it is where we have the main interchange of energy with our aura, the energy field that surrounds us. Energy flows from the outside world into our aura and we are continually sensing energies in our surroundings. This energy flows through our chakras into our body where energetic information is processed, producing feelings and emotional responses within us.

Most energy-healing modalities focus energy through the chakras and Crystal Reiki Healing is no different in this respect. The big difference is the boost to healing that crystals and Reiki offer each other.

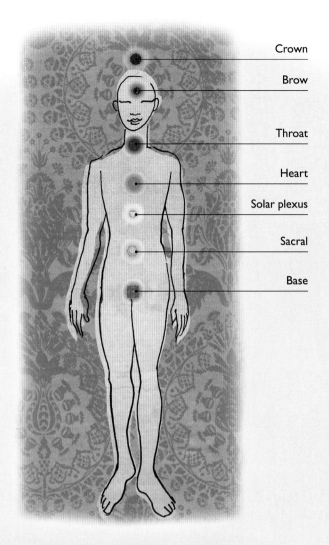

Crown

Brow

Throat

Heart

Solar plexus

Sacral

Base

LOCATING THE CHAKRAS

Crown chakra—on the top of the head

Brow chakra (also known as the third-eye chakra)—in the center of the forehead, above the eyebrows

Throat chakra—in the center of the throat

Heart chakra—in the center of the chest

Solar plexus chakra—behind the soft cartilage at the bottom of the breast bone

Sacral chakra—just below the belly button. Try placing your thumb on your belly button with your palm on your tummy—your sacral chakra will be under the palm of your hand

Base chakra—at the coccyx at the base of the spine

TRADITIONAL CHAKRA CRYSTALS

Although you can work with any crystal at any chakra point as required, it is traditional to connect crystals to chakras by color. As depicted in the illustration (see page 19), you can see the colors of the chakras follow the colors of the rainbow, from the base up to the crown: red, orange, yellow, green, blue, indigo, and violet. An easy starting point is to work with red jasper or garnet, carnelian or orange calcite, citrine or yellow jasper, malachite or aventurine, blue lace agate or blue chalcedony, lapis lazuli or sodalite, and amethyst or lepidolite.

THE CRYSTAL CHAKRA SET

CHAKRA	ASSOCIATED CRYSTALS			
Crown	Amethyst		Lepidolite	
Brow	Lapis lazuli		Soladite	
Throat	Blue lace agate		Blue chalcedony	
Heart	Malachite		Aventurine	
Solar plexus	Citrine		Yellow jasper	
Sacral	Carnelian		Orange calcite	
Base	Red jasper		Garnet	

QUARTZ MASTER CRYSTAL

You will also need a quartz master crystal, which is a large natural crystal with a termination (point). It should be large enough to hold in your hand, with the bottom touching the minor chakra in your palm and the termination protruding out of your hand. A comfortable size for most people is 3–6 inches (7–15 cm). Too small and it is too fiddly; too large and it is too heavy to work with.

CRYSTAL REIKI GUIDES

Generally, spirit guides can come in many guises. They might be relatives or close friends who have passed, wise experts from a previous age, spiritual leaders, or simply spirits from another time. Some people also suggest they might come from other planets or dimensions. Wherever they hail from, they bring knowledge and guidance to help you on your path. Everyone has guides around them.

Crystal guides have a special interest in crystal healing and the mineral kingdom, Reiki guides in Reiki healing. When you start to work with crystals or Reiki, you enhance the connection with these guides. Your Crystal Reiki guide will be interested in helping you combine these two modalities for healing and increasing your spiritual awareness. When you first discover a new guide, they often appear as a blue light hovering nearby until you acknowledge them.

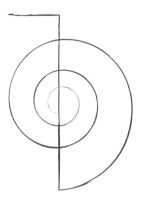

Cho Ku Rei

Sei He Ki

Reiki symbols

Definition of "symbol"[1]:

1. a mark or character used as a conventional representation of an object, function, or process, e.g. the letter or letters standing for a chemical element or a character in musical notation.

2. a thing that represents or stands for something else, especially a material object representing something abstract.

We use symbols in our daily lives—for example, +, ×, and %. Each is instantly recognized and understood. However, they are all representations of complicated mathematical processes. We don't need to explain or even understand the calculation to find the answer—we simply follow the process. We are attuned to these symbols in school. Without a basic knowledge of mathematics, these symbols are useless squiggles on paper or screen.

In the same way, there are sacred Reiki symbols: Cho Ku Rei, Sei He Ki, Hon Sha Ze Sho Nen, Dai Ko Myo, and Raku. Cho Ku Rei, Sei He Ki, Hon Sha Ze Sho Nen and the main version of Dai Ko Myo all come from Usui Reiki. Raku and the second version of Dai Ko Myo are "Tibetan" symbols. I have put Tibetan in quotation marks because it is almost certain that these do not originate in Tibet at all but have been linked with the country; they probably originate from Chinese shamanism.

All the symbols convey function and process, but also something abstract, hard to define, and almost impossible to explain. They represent the essence of ki, universal life force energy. Whenever any symbol is used and reused, drawn and redrawn, it accumulates power. Once you are attuned at Reiki

Level 2 and above, every time you draw a symbol it takes on not only your energy but a little of the force from every time it has ever been drawn by any person practicing Reiki in the world. Cho Ku Rei and the Tibetan symbols have a natural power that can be accessed even if you have not been attuned.

The Reiki symbols do not only have a healing function, representing a therapeutic process and carrying energy; they are also keys to the doors of awakening and higher consciousness. They elevate your awareness and bring about manifestation. What Usui Sensei discovered on Mount Kurama were the tools to attune people to ki. It's just like tuning in a radio—when you find the station, the music plays. These symbolic keys connect and tune you in to the universal life force itself.

In the past there has been much discussion about whether these symbols should be secret as well as sacred. However, circumstances have overtaken these discussions and as they are readily visible all over the internet today there is no point in taking this debate further. What remains vitally important is that these symbols are sacred. If you treat them as such, they will help and support your practice, if you treat them otherwise, they won't. Please give them respect.

Because the symbols are drawn by hand, there is variation in their style. The depictions that follow are the ones I have always used; if yours vary, it doesn't make them wrong. Try the ones on the following pages and if yours are different, use the version you feel comfortable with. Intent is paramount when working with the symbols.

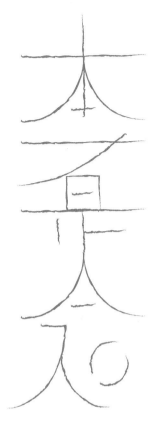

Hon Sha Ze Sho Nen

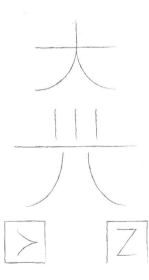

Dai Ko Myo

Raku—Lightning bolt

Raku—Fire serpent

Tibetan Dai Ko Myo

WAYS OF CREATING SYMBOLS

- Drawing: draw the symbol on paper with pen or pencil, or in the air with your palm or finger—or your nose! You can even draw the symbols on the roof of your mouth with your tongue. Drawing the symbols in the air with a crystal wand or selenite "pencil" wand will amplify their energy.

- Visualization: picture the symbol in your mind. The easiest way to do this is to draw the symbol on paper and look at the image until it is imprinted in your mind, then close your eyes and hold the image in your memory. With a little practice you'll be able to visualize the image for long periods of time and you won't need to draw it; it will simply appear in your mind as you think about it.

- With crystals: create the symbols from tumble-polished stones or crystals.

However you choose to invoke the symbols, you should chant the name of each symbol three times as you call on it (three being the number of manifestation). Always remember if you treat these symbols as sacred once you are attuned to them, they will greatly enhance everything you do.

CHO KU REI—THE POWER SYMBOL

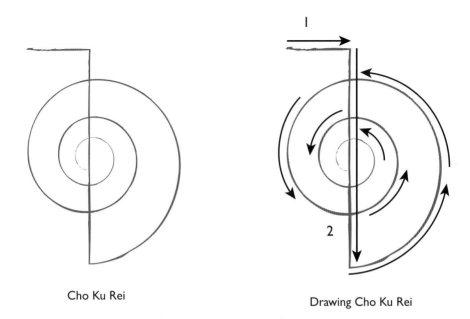

Cho Ku Rei

Drawing Cho Ku Rei

Cho Ku Rei is known as the power symbol because it's like a switch that turns on the Reiki power. It jump-starts a treatment and can seal it at the end. Because it focuses energy, it can direct extra Reiki to any specific area of the body. It can also act as a shield to prevent external energy from affecting a healing room and energy released by clients from spilling out.

Cho Ku Rei is protective for you and your partner, children, friends, animals, home, and car—anyone and anything that is important to you. It offers protection from the energy your clients release during a treatment, psychic attack, accidents, and arguments.

You can cleanse crystals energetically by drawing Cho Ku Rei over them with your hands. And you can also do the same with food and drink.

The symbol enhances your confidence in stressful situations such as exams, interviews, journeys, and operations. Remember that you can use the symbol before, during, and after any event.

Cho Ku Rei acts like a switch for all the other symbols and adds even more power to them. Even if not attuned, this symbol offers a noticeable amount of power (which increases greatly after attunement).

DRAWING CHO KU REI

The way each symbol is drawn matters as it alters its frequency and effect. Cho Ku Rei can be drawn clockwise, counterclockwise, from the top down, and from the center outward. Traditionally, it should be drawn from the top down with a counterclockwise spiral. This increases the flow of energy where it is being channeled. Drawing from the center outward decreases the flow of energy and can be beneficial if you want to remove negative energy from a client or room.

POWER YOURSELF WITH CHO KU REI

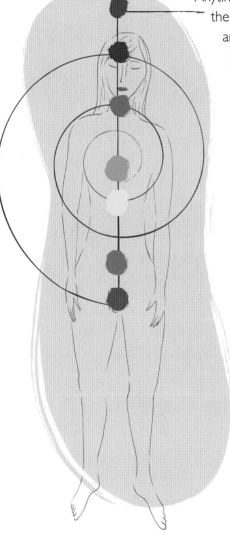

Anytime you need a bit of a boost, try this. It is especially useful at the start of the day, before treating others, before teaching a class and doing attunements, or just because you like the feeling it gives you!

1. Hold your quartz master crystal (see page 21) in both hands and visualize Cho Ku Rei inside the crystal. See it glowing, as if it is drawn in a violet flame. With the crystal's termination pointing toward the palm of one of your hands, draw Cho Ku Rei in the air with the crystal just above your palm and chant the name three times. Repeat this on your other hand.

2. Again with your master crystal, draw the symbol over each of your seven major chakras, starting with the base and working up to the crown, each time chanting the name of the symbol three times.

3. Finally as shown in the illustration, draw a big Cho Ku Rei symbol over your body with your master crystal, beginning by tracing a line with your crystal above your head from your right, then down the center of your body to your base chakra. From there, draw a clockwise spiral through your chakras: base up to crown, down to sacral and up to brow, round to your solar plexus then up to your throat, and finally down to your heart to complete the symbol. When this is seen on you, as if you are looking in a mirror, it completes the counterclockwise spiral.

SEI HE KI—THE MENTAL/EMOTIONAL SYMBOL

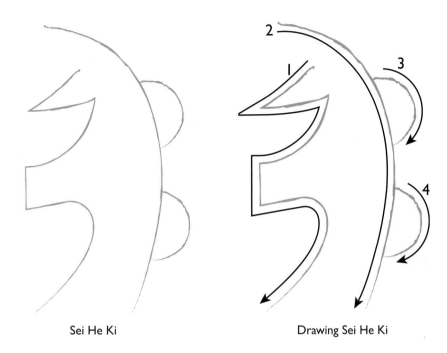

Sei He Ki   Drawing Sei He Ki

Sei He Ki is called the mental/emotional symbol because its energy is directed in these fields, but you could also call it the stress symbol. This is important because almost all physical injuries and illnesses are directly related to stress. We know that stressed people have a weakened immune system and are likely to catch any bug that's going around. We're also aware of many 21st-century illnesses and conditions that are directly stress-related or greatly exacerbated by it, such as Crohn's disease, heart conditions, psoriasis, and migraine. But what are often overlooked are the direct stress causes of physical injury. Take, for example, the person who is taken to the emergency department with a broken leg because she has been run over by a bus. There can be many causes, but unless it has been a freak accident, we have to ask why she was so stressed out that she didn't notice a very large bus when she crossed the road. She must have been under considerable stress. And the hospital is great at fixing the body, setting bones, and prescribing painkillers; but unless the stress is dealt with, she will just walk under the next proverbial bus. This is why Sei He Ki is so important in Crystal Reiki Healing: we are always looking to heal the cause of any condition, so it doesn't reoccur.

Sei He Ki is said to balance right- and left-brain activity, bringing harmony and peace. It is particularly helpful for healing relationship issues, anxiety, nervousness, and panic attacks, as well as fear, depression, sadness, and grief. It also helps memory and can be applied in the treatment of dementia-related conditions.

Sei He Ki enhances affirmations, purifies and brings together energy that is pulling you in different directions, and guards against negative emotions. It is good for any shock or trauma, can help potentize medicines, food, and alternative remedies, aids animal healing and letting go of the past, and can feel like a big hug when you just need someone to hold you. For calming shock, draw Sei He Ki in the air with an aqua aura crystal—this can bring a rapid release of the trauma.

This symbol is most potent once attuned to at least Reiki Level 2, although some power can be sensed if used before attunement or at Level 1.

DRAWING SEI HE KI

This symbol is drawn in four strokes. Start with the left stroke, going downward from the top, followed by the right, again from top to bottom. Then, each with a single downward stroke, draw the top loop and finally the bottom loop.

LET GO OF STRESS AND WORRIES WITH SEI HE KI

You will need a large piece of paper and a pen or pencil, ideally in green, violet, or blue. Avoid using a black pen, because black absorbs energy and we want to let energy go.

1. Find a quiet, calm place where you can sit comfortably. In your mind, visualize Sei He Ki clearly drawn in green, violet, or blue. Hold this mental image for as long as you can. With practice you will be able to do this for longer.

2. Now draw the image on your paper and focus your mind on anything or anyone that is causing you stress or worrying you. Picture distinctly this event, issue, or person, or if you find it difficult to visualize, then simply describe it in words in your mind. Take a really deep breath and breathe this image or thought into the symbol you have drawn. Imagine your Sei He Ki absorbing your worry or stress and transmuting it into Reiki, and watch that Reiki flowing to the source of your problem and surrounding it with Sei He Ki symbols, dancing in a violet Reiki sea and dissolving the issue in your mind.

You can repeat this process for any number of things that are worrying you.

HON SHA ZE SHO NEN—THE DISTANCE SYMBOL

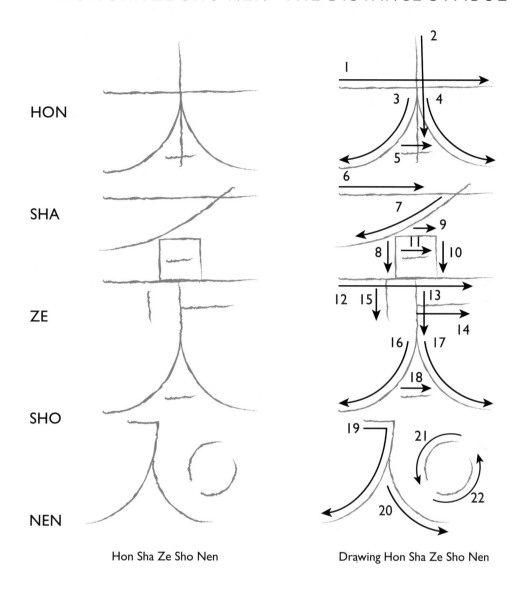

HON

SHA

ZE

SHO

NEN

Hon Sha Ze Sho Nen   Drawing Hon Sha Ze Sho Nen

Some people can feel quite challenged by this symbol, and some are confused by its use. It is commonly known as the distance symbol, but, in reality, it isn't just connected to distance as it transcends time and space, and it can help with everything, because everything is within the time-space continuum. Although this symbol is employed in distant healing, it also has a place in almost any healing scenario. Remember our friend with the broken leg who was hit by the bus (see page 27? Well, you could take a good guess that her stress was related to either something in the past or something in the future. In either case, Hon Sha Ze Sho Nen would be used in her healing session. How many of your own issues are linked to the past? Are you worried about the future? The "future" includes both the next five minutes and what will happen to the planet well after we are all gone, as well as what lies in between.

This symbol is most potent once attuned to at least Reiki Level 2, although some power can be sensed if used before attunement or at Level 1.

DRAWING HON SHA ZE SHO NEN

This is the most complicated symbol to draw, so, as with the other symbols, I've provided a diagram (see page 29) that shows the order in which to draw all the strokes.

HEAL THE PAST WITH HON SHA ZE SHO NEN

1. Sit quietly and focus your mind. Take a pen and paper and write down any stresses in your life. Now look at these and see which ones are connected to the past.

2. Once you have noted these issues, call in your Crystal Reiki Guide and any other guides who might help (see page 21). Then take your quartz master crystal (see page 21) and with it draw Hon Sha Ze Sho Nen over each problem on your list, intoning the name of the symbol three times. Ask for Reiki to flow back in time and space to the cause of each one and to heal *all* the people concerned (and any animals—i.e. all living things). It is important to send the healing to everyone, even if you feel challenged by sending good energy to someone you feel has wronged you. You must do this to heal a situation in the past, because otherwise some of the energy remains trapped and will continue to hold you back.

3. Once you have completed this process for each item on your list, thank your quartz master crystal and your guides for helping you. Take three deep breaths, and as you breathe out, know that you have changed the energy tied to this moment.

DISTANT HEALING WITH HON SHA ZE SHO NEN

You can use Hon Sha Ze Sho Nen to connect to anyone or anything anywhere in the world, and for this reason the symbol is always associated with distant healing—sending healing energy to those not with you (see page 93). Although there are many Reiki ways of sending distant healing, there is a neat trick of working with a crystal ball to add oomph to your work!

1. Buy, beg, or borrow (long term) a notepad and pen. Write on the front the words "Healing Book" and inside it start adding the names of anyone you want to send healing to. Some people like to write one name per page, others prefer to simply list them together. You might choose to add more details about them, such as the condition that needs healing, their age, or where they live. You can add as many or as few details as you feel happy with. You can add more names as you go along.

2. Call on your Crystal Reiki guide (see page 21) and any other guides you want to help you.

3. Hold your quartz crystal ball in both hands and either let Reiki flow into it or, if you are attuned to Reiki Level 2 or 3, visualize each symbol in a violet haze inside the crystal. Place the crystal ball to one side.

4. Connect to your quartz master crystal (see page 21) and draw Hon Sha Ze Sho Nen over the book with it. Then place both hands on the book to let Reiki flow and heal the book, as if you were giving a treatment to a person.

5. Lay your book closed flat on a table or shelf—anywhere it won't be disturbed—and place your crystal ball charged with Reiki on top. You might need a stand to support it; if you haven't got a stand, you can use a ring, small cushion pad, or sticky tack to hold it in place. Draw Hon Sha Ze Sho Nen with your quartz master crystal over the crystal ball and book. Thank your guide.

It is always best to do things in a regular pattern and sending distant healing is no exception. Find a time you can send it either daily or weekly. It's nice to do this with friends in a group, too. If you cannot be together in the same place, simply arrange a "Crystal Reiki Healing meet up" for a specific time when everyone draws Hon Sha Ze Sho Nen at the same moment. This will connect your energies together, no matter how far away you are physically from each other.

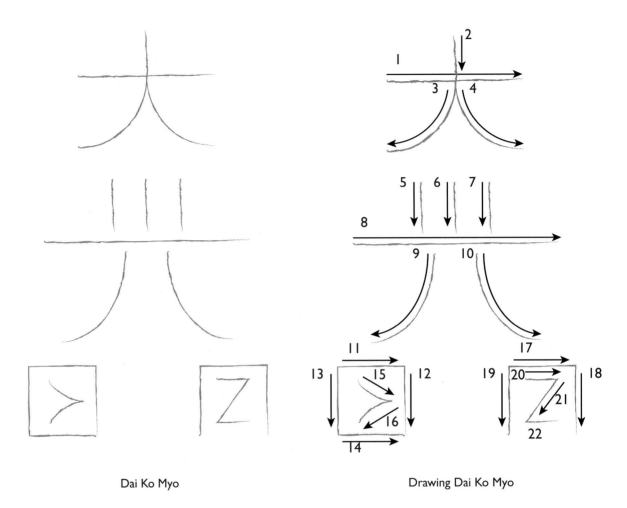

Dai Ko Myo   Drawing Dai Ko Myo

This is the key symbol for attuning students to Reiki and, like Sei He Ki and Hon Sha Ze Sho Nen—it only holds its full power once you have been attuned to it. As with the other symbols, there are variations in how this symbol is drawn in different Reiki systems. However, its purpose remains the same.

Dai Ko Myo can be loosely translated as "Great being of the universe, shine on me, be my friend." A Zen Buddhist understanding relates to the true Buddha nature of man; the experience of enlightenment—"Treasure house of the great beaming light"[2]. This also would tie in with Usui Sensei's experience on Mount

Kurama. The essence of the symbol is about energy emanating from the divine. This corresponds with the descriptions of the wonderful intense feelings reported by students receiving the gift of their Reiki Master Teacher attunement.

Dai Ko Myo intensely focuses Reiki, not only as is required for passing on attunements, but also for all levels of healing and manifestation. Ask and the universe will provide, but please do be careful what you ask for, because you might just get it… and it could turn out to be too much for you to handle.

DRAWING DAI KO MYO

This symbol is drawn with 22 distinct lines—see the diagram for guidance.

SWITCH YOUR HEALING HANDS ON WITH DAI KO MYO

This is an excellent exercise to try before giving a treatment or attunement. Draw the Master symbol with your finger on the palm of one hand, then repeat with the other hand. Clap your hands together three times whilst chanting the name of the symbol. Feel the energy in your hands. This offers a fairly instant effect, especially if you have been attuned.

THINK SYMBOLS

Practice drawing symbols until you think them and see them automatically in your mind and in front of you in the air. Then they become magic. If you see someone in an emotional state and think Sei He Ki and see Sei He Ki, the symbol does the rest as it floats to the person and eases their heart. If you see someone who is feeling low, think Cho Ku Rei and see the symbol go to them.

You'll see the reaction of people to these symbols almost instantly, just like magic—symbol magic.

RAKU—THE GROUNDING SYMBOL

Raku—Lightning bolt

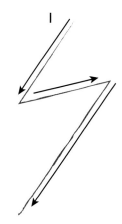

Drawing Raku—Lightning bolt

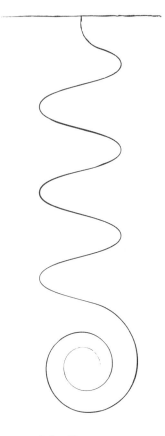

Raku: Fire serpent

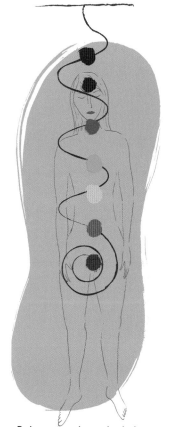

Raku going through chakras

Raku is both a grounding and a connecting symbol and is presented in two ways. Its simplest depiction is the lightning bolt, which can ground a client after a treatment. You can create a crystal Raku out of hematite stones under your therapy bed to create a grounding experience for clients (see page 145).

The other form of the symbol is the fire serpent. In this presentation, Raku is connected to the raising of kundalini energy from its root at the base chakra. Kundalini is the source of primal energy and consciousness that we are born with. It comes coiled like a serpent at the base of the spine and can be awakened by working with Raku, among other methods.

Raku is useful at the end of a treatment or attunement, or at any time when someone might experience an energy shift which could leave them feeling spaced-out. It can also be helpful for you if you feel any situation is spiraling out of control or people are panicking or hysterical: it shifts the energy, which results in a calming effect.

DRAWING RAKU

The lightning bolt is drawn from the top downward. The fire serpent form is also usually drawn from the top downward, with each bend going through a chakra and culminating with the spiral at the base chakra. However, it can also be drawn from the base up to raise the kundalini energy.

GROUNDING WITH RAKU

As already mentioned, the Raku symbols work very well with hematite. This exercise offers a simple way to ground yourself whenever needed.

1. Take two hematite stones, about 1–2 inches (2.5–5 cm) in size, one in each hand. Stand with your feet under your shoulders, keeping your knees soft to take the pressure off them. Close your eyes and imagine there is an anchor in each of your hands. Visualize this falling to the floor and going into the earth, deeper and deeper down into the ground.

2. Now draw two lightning bolts with the hematite stones over the ground and feel y our feet sinking slowly into the floor. Take three slow deep breaths and open your eyes.

TIBETAN DAI KO MYO

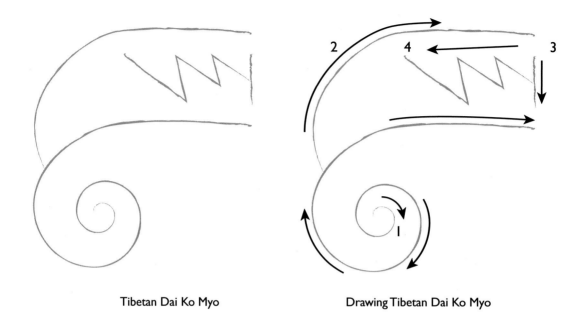

Tibetan Dai Ko Myo   Drawing Tibetan Dai Ko Myo

This version of Dai Ko Myo is a pictogram of a ram's horn with a lightning bolt being carried within it. Tibetan Dai Ko Myo can be used to energetically clear a space before a treatment or any ceremony or ritual. The lightning flash dispels any negative energy that is present. The cleansing process is important at the start of attunements and treatments. It can be used to clear energy blocks during a treatment and cleanse a room, crystals, and anything else you wish. This is a good symbol to depict in crystals in your treatment room to keep cleansing the energy.

DRAWING TIBETAN DAI KO MYO

This symbol is drawn with three lines. Start the first line at the center of the spiral and draw to the end of the spiral. Then draw the outer line to the left, creating a vessel looking similar to a ram's horn. Finally, from the top, draw the lightning bolt coming down into the horn.

CLEAR YOUR AURA OF UNHELPFUL ENERGY WITH TIBETAN DAI KO MYO

We interact with energy sources all the time. Whether that's people we meet, clients, friends, lovers, computers, or contacts on social media, and they *all* influence us. We take on some of their energy. Sometimes this is wonderful and gives us that amazing "up" feeling. But other times this external energy can be unhelpful and bring us down, so it is useful to clear the aura of this unwanted energy. You can repeat this exercise as often as you like during the day.

1. Draw Tibetan Dai Ko Myo in the air in front of you, chanting its name three times. Take a deep in-breath and step into the space where you drew the symbol.

2. Hold your breath for a moment, then imagine you are breathing out any energy from your aura that's unhelpful. Notice how you feel.

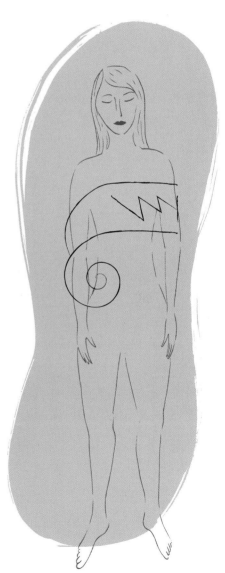

How to Reiki a crystal

As I said at the beginning, crystals love Reiki, and when you add Reiki to a crystal, its energy sparkles! Because crystals are sensitive to other energies, they amplify and hold Reiki, making it more powerful and portable. So, before you work with crystals in Crystal Reiki Healing treatments or give a crystal as a gift to a friend, Reiki your crystals—that is, charge or infuse them with Reiki power.

To Reiki a crystal, follow these steps:

1. Turn Reiki on. There are many ways taught to switch your Reiki energy on and whatever works for you is fine. I like just saying "Reiki on!" as an affirmation. However, once you are attuned to Reiki and you even think about healing, your Reiki energy will flow. Call in your Crystal Reiki guides, too (see page 21).

2. Tune into your chosen crystal: follow the steps on page 47, but it doesn't have to be a quartz crystal.

3. Sit quietly and hold your crystal with Reiki flowing through you until you feel the crystal is filled with Reiki—this usually takes a few minutes. If you're unsure if your crystal is filled up, you can ask your pendulum for confirmation (see pages 42–43).

4. Your crystal is Reiki-ready. Thank your guides.

PROGRAMMING CRYSTALS WITH REIKI

Because crystals can hold energy, they can also be programmed for specific purposes. And as they can be charged with Reiki for a prolonged period of time, you can create a portable and sustainable Reiki treatment for someone even if they are not attuned to Reiki themselves. You can send a friend or relative in need a crystal infused with Reiki or a client can carry crystals charged with Reiki for a boost between treatment sessions.

1. What do you want to achieve? Decide what outcome you wish for before you start. It may be healing something specific, such as a part of the body or a medical condition, or more for general health. As you will see later, it may also be to help you toward a life goal or something on your spiritual path, or simply to make your life a little easier by finding an easy parking space at the supermarket. Whatever it is will

influence which crystal you choose to help you, whether consciously or not.

2. Turn Reiki on and tune into your crystal (see steps 1 and 2 on page 38).

3. As you sit quietly and hold your crystal with Reiki flowing through you, ask in your mind what you want the crystal to help with, and send out your request to the universe. Whatever it is, visualize it in your mind as completed. For example, if it is to speed recovery, picture yourself (or your client, friend, or relative) completely better and fully healed. (If you are attuned to Reiki Level 2 or above, you can also add the appropriate symbols to this programming. Always include Hon Sha Ze Sho Nen to surpass time and distance when programming a crystal; it is up to you to decide which other symbols are most appropriate.)

4. Thank your crystal for helping you, as well as your Crystal Reiki guides and any other spirits or angels you have invoked.

5. Place the crystal somewhere it won't be disturbed to carry on working its crystal magic or give it to your client or friend.

Repeat this process daily until the outcome is achieved. Some things happen quickly, some slowly. When the desired effect is fulfilled, you can cleanse the crystal and work with it again for another task. You might find that some crystals prefer to help with healing, while others might like to aid your lifestyle. Some crystals are very specialized, a little like a brain surgeon: brilliant at what they do, but don't ask them to change a washer in a faucet. Others may be more like a Jack of all trades and can turn their molecules to most things.

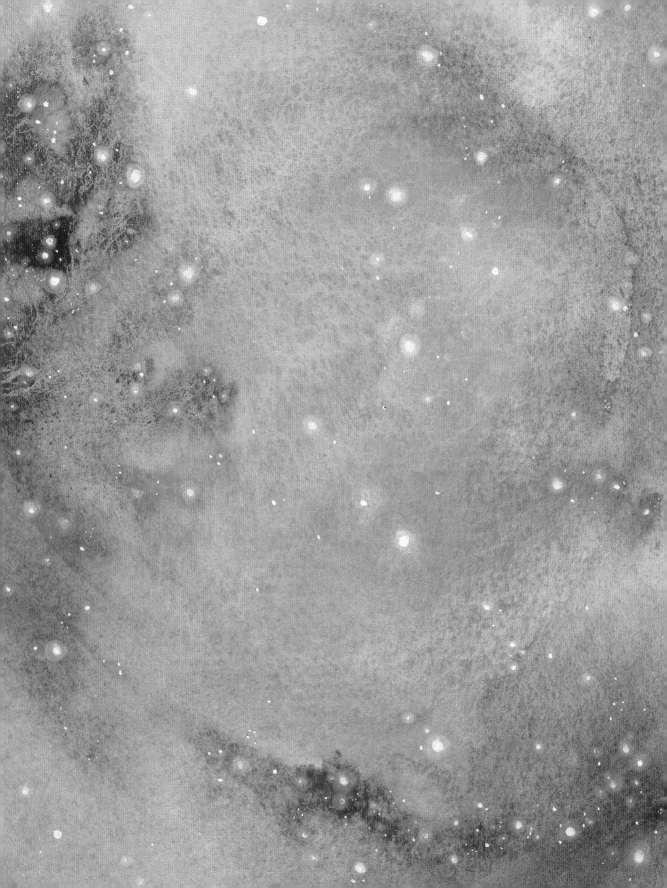

chapter 2

preparation FOR Crystal Reiki Healing

Discover how to get yourself and your environment ready for healing both yourself and others, including ways to select your crystals, what to consider before performing treatments, and techniques to mentally prepare yourself.

selecting crystals

You might want to select crystals for many reasons: to work with in Crystal Reiki treatments, for self-healing, inspiration, or productivity, to help with problems, or to bring love and happiness into your life. You can use these methods to help you choose a suitable variety of crystal, such as amethyst or ruby, or to help you listen to a group of the same type of crystal to see which individual one wants to help you. Either way, once chosen you can look it up in the Crystal Finder (see page 105) to see its associations and how best to work with it.

CHOOSING CRYSTALS INTUITIVELY

There is an old crystal saying: "If you are drawn to a crystal, you need it!" And by and large this is true. We are all intuitive and naturally know what we need. I'd like to change the words just a little to: "If you notice a crystal, you need it." It's not only the sparkling ones waving across the room and drawing you to them, but also the ones you don't like. The ones you feel you cannot touch or look at, or even go anywhere near them. The ones that make you ill at ease, nervous, and nauseous. The energy from such a crystal is reaching

deep inside you and touching something you don't want to acknowledge. It will make you feel uncomfortable. However, choose this crystal and it will help you to shed whatever is holding you down, emotionally, physically, mentally, or spiritually. These are the crystals that produce life-changing energy shifts. The journey may not always be fun, but the destination is worth it. Such discomforts never last long. Probably a few hours, a day or two, or a week or two at the very most. The key is to keep going once you've started. Doing Crystal Reiki Healing self-treatments (see page 68) every day will help to speed this process.

Two different lapis
lazuli crystals

WORKING WITH A CRYSTAL PENDULUM

A crystal pendulum can be an excellent instrument to aid your intuitive development and gain confidence in your abilities, and a valuable tool on your Crystal Reiki Healing journey. It can help you to feel and "see" your inner vision. Your pendulum offers a reflection of your internal feelings. We all have an inner pendulum. Some call it a gut feeling, intuition, or an inner knowing. It's the bit inside you that says "yes" or "no" to everything, all day long, every moment. It resides in your sacral chakra (see page 19) and has two distinct reactions. Everyone has experienced these, but we often only notice them at the extremes. One is a sinking feeling, where your stomach feels like it is dropping to your feet. This is the "Get me out of here!" or "I'm really scared, I want to leave NOW!" sensation. And we all know the "yes" feeling too—the euphoric inner high, the "Wow! This is amazing!" or "Love—true, real love." It's the feeling coming up into your chest, into your heart, from your navel.

A pendulum moves in different directions, but for each individual it always moves the same way to say "yes" and a different way to say "no." When you see the pendulum moving in front of you, it is mirroring your inner feelings and you can begin to get in touch with your inner pendulum moving up and down inside you. Working with a pendulum in this way is known as dowsing, and it is one of the oldest forms of divination.

CHOOSING A PENDULUM

Select a pendulum, hold it in your hands, and allow your Reiki energy to flow into it. (If you are at Reiki Level 2, you can also visualize Hon Sha Ze Sho Nen (see page 29), the "distance" symbol, to connect the Reiki energy to your crystal in time and space to see the answers you need.) Then hold the pendulum's chain and ask it two simple questions which have definitive answers—for example, "Am I a woman?"—and as you ask this your pendulum will move. Maybe back and forth, side to side, or in clockwise or counterclockwise circles. Whatever it does will represent your "yes" or "no." Now ask the opposite question—in this case, "Am I a man?"—and observe your pendulum move in a different way. This is the pendulum showing you the opposite answer. Now you know your yes and no responses, you can ask your pendulum, "Are you a good pendulum for me to work with?" If it says "no," then pop it back and try another! When it says "Yes," you have a friend for life.

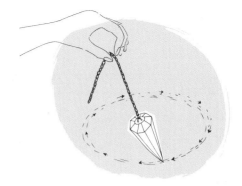

HOW YOUR PENDULUM HELPS

I've always worked with a pendulum, relying heavily on it when I began crystal healing, and even now sometimes falling back on it for confirmation or clarification. For example, sometimes I know a client needs a particular crystal because it seems to be sparkling and waving at me, but I have no idea where it needs to go on their body! The pendulum always works. I have three pendulums: one made from lapis lazuli for healings, a second made from amethyst for teaching, and a third natural citrine one for personal questions.

Your pendulum is a powerful tool. Every time you ask it a question, it is mirroring your inner self. You already know the answer. Your pendulum is helping to teach you how to connect to your inner being—or, more accurately, remind you, because as a child, you were likely told by parents, teachers, and society in general to ignore it. Now is the time to remember and tap into the innate knowledge and wisdom that is within us all.

If you treat your pendulum as a spiritual tool, it will always give you the right answer (whether you like it or not!). If you treat it as a game, then it will treat you in the same way. And if you keep asking the same question, it will get bored and start giving you different answers. And pendulums always answer in the moment. They do not predict the future. So, if you ask, "Will I get together with 20 friends for a reunion dinner next year?" the answer your pendulum would give is not a prediction of what will happen next year, but a report of what you and your 20 friends currently intend to do next year.

As you continue your Reiki journey and become attuned to higher levels, be aware that the attunement process alters your energy and vibration, so may result in your pendulum swinging differently for "yes" and "no" responses. Recheck your yes and no movements occasionally, and especially during the 21-day period after any Reiki attunement.

TREATING YOUR PENDULUM
AS A SPIRITUAL TOOL

Sometime soon after I started working as a crystal healer in the early 1990s, I was interviewed by a newspaper journalist and she was really taken with pendulums, so much so that she bought one for herself.

She phoned me the next day in tears. She told me that when she went into work that morning, she took her pendulum and was demonstrating its magical powers to everyone in the office. Then someone suggested they should bet on a horse race. Everyone put a dollar into a pot. They asked the pendulum which horse would win and it guided them to a horse in the first race of the day. They placed the bet. The horse won! "Wow! Let's do it again!" they said. Now, this time everyone in the office put $50 into the pot. The room went still as her pendulum picked another horse… only this time, it lost. So then her co-workers were furious!

I explained that the first time the amount of money was really insignificant to everyone and the pendulum treated the exercise as a valid way to show it worked. A spiritual quest. The second time was plain greed and not spiritual at all, so the pendulum treated them as such and played a game. Ha ha ha, very funny—not for her.

I told her to ask everyone in the office to put another $50 into the pot, but this time to agree on a charity to which they would give all the winnings and the stake money before asking the pendulum to choose another winner. She dowsed the runners with her pendulum in the last race of the day, picked a horse… and it won.

The moral of the (true) story is to treat your pendulum with respect and it will always guide you well; treat it as a game and it will treat you in the same way.

PENDULUM DOWSING WITH REIKI

Now you have tuned into your pendulum, try this exercise to observe the added effect of crystal and Reiki energy.

1. Place your hand palm facing down on a large piece of paper. Hold your pendulum about an inch or two (2.5–5cm) over the ends of your fingers and ask, "Are you in my aura?" It will show you a "yes" indication. Hold this question in your mind and slowly move your pendulum away from your hand until its direction changes to a "no" response. Mark this place on the paper with a pencil.

2. Place a quartz crystal under the palm of your hand and repeat the exercise. You will find that the positive response continues further from your hand, showing that your aura has almost instantly become larger (perhaps beyond your piece of paper).

3. Repeat this again with the crystal under your hand, but this time allow your Reiki energy to flow through your hand. (If you are attuned to Reiki Level 2 or above you can visualize the Reiki symbols in the palm of your hand, too.) Again, you will find that your aura has become even larger.

This can be a fun exercise to do with a partner or friend. Hold the pendulum by their heart and move it away in front of them until it changes its response. Then do the same with them holding a quartz crystal to their heart. And then once more with them holding the crystal but also adding Reiki. If they are attuned to Reiki, they can let it flow through them or visualize the symbols. If they're not attuned, you can send Reiki to them—it works just as well. Make sure you have plenty of room in front of them as Reiki can expand the aura dramatically!

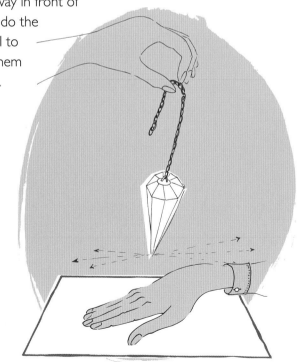

SELECTING CRYSTALS WITH REIKI

Once you're attuned to Reiki, it will activate your intuition and can be focused to help you select crystals instead of using a pendulum if you prefer.

1. Place a selection of crystals on the table in front of you. It is easiest if they are in a horizontal line to begin with, but once you get the hang of this method they can be in a random pile, a bowl, or anywhere you can reach.

2. Take a quiet moment to focus yourself. Place your hands in Gassho (see page 58), focus where your middle fingers meet, and welcome your Reiki Guide in (see page 21). You might like to consciously think or say, "Reiki on."

3. Place either or both of your hands a couple of inches (5 cm) above the line of crystals, moving slowly over each one from right to left. Be aware of any changes. It is usual that above one (or more) of the crystals your hand(s) will experience a temperature change, becoming warm or cool, so these are the crystals to choose. You are sensing the energy of the crystals and your Reiki hands are reacting to the ones you need.

You can use this method to select crystals for yourself, family, friends, and clients. It also works well for choosing crystals to send distant healing (see page 93).

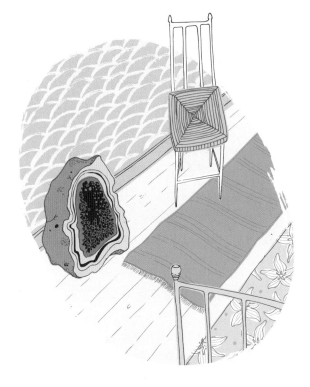

creating a sacred Crystal Reiki Healing space

It is important that your healing room is a sanctuary, for you and for anyone else you may treat there. You should enjoy being in your special space and the energy you create inside it. Spend some time there when you are not performing healing. Meditate (see page 58) and generally enjoy the energy you have created in your room. Ideally it should be a safe—practically and in feeling—clean and cleansed room which is used solely for healing (or healing/teaching type-events). This is not always possible, but a ritual to cleanse and dedicate the room will be useful if the room has many uses (see page 52).

A CLEAN ROOM

This is an absolute and a surprisingly overlooked consideration. Some people are so concerned with cleansing everything energetically they forget about the basics: vacuum or sweep the floors, dust every surface, and get a feather duster in the corners. Clean your mat or therapy bed and make sure you have fresh clean covers. Then lie on your mat on the floor or therapy couch and look up. Now remove these cobwebs, too!

ENERGETIC CLEANSING

Once the room is clean, you can start to focus on cleansing the space energetically. I love using tingsha (Tibetan bells) to cleanse my healing room or any other space, crystals, myself—basically, anything and everything! Ring them in the middle of the room and then around the edge of the room, paying particular attention to any corners and also over your crystals and mat or therapy bed. When you clink them together, the sound waves they generate literally vibrate and shake the molecules of the item they are cleansing, which releases any trapped energy. Bells symbolize beginnings and endings; for example, birth, marriage, and death are all signaled by ringing. They summon people to events, such as dinner or a church service, they alert us to someone at the front door, and they warn us of danger. According to Tibetan Buddhist belief, ringing bells shows love to the Buddha and brings good karma.

When I need to cleanse lots of crystals or a larger space, such as somewhere I'm teaching a class or workshop, I will work with a crystal singing bowl to cleanse the space and everything in it. Crystal singing bowls are made from quartz crystal and are often tuned to a specific note that resonates with a particular chakra. These can be very powerful healing instruments. They produce a pure resonant tone, which is perfect for cleansing, relaxing, meditation, and healing. You can strike a crystal singing bowl like a gong, or tone it giving a constant sound. You can also use bells, gongs, Tibetan singing bowls, chimes, and drums to cleanse energy.

Crystals such as amethyst, quartz, and selenite can help to keep the energy refreshed. Place large pieces of these crystals where you can, especially near your working crystals, under the therapy bed, and in any seated area where you take information from people you are treating.

Tibetan Dai Ko Myo (see page 36) can be used energetically to clear a space before a treatment or any ceremony or ritual.

CRYSTAL REIKI WATER

It is good to drink this any time, but especially after a Crystal Reiki Healing treatment and Reiki attunements. Essentially this is a crystal elixir with a Reiki boost.

Place a quartz crystal in a glass or pitcher of water. Place your hands either side and send Reiki to the water. Draw Tibetan Dai Ko Myo and Cho Ku Rei symbols over the water (see pages 36 and 25). Ideally prepare the water at least an hour before drinking. You can also do this the night before you need it.

COMFORT

The most important thing is that you are comfortable, whether healing alone or treating others. So, the temperature should be as you like it, as should ventilation, any music you wish to play, scents from incense or oils, the crystals around your room, and the colors you choose. The same goes for the clothes you wear. If you're treating others and feel at ease in therapy "whites," wear them, but if you feel better in flowing clothing or a T-shirt and jeans, that's great, as long as whatever you wear is clean and comfortable.

Always have drinking water, or ideally Crystal Reiki water (see above), available for both you and anyone else you are treating. Healing can be very hot and thirsty work, even on cold days. Some people get very hot and dry throated when receiving healing. Always offer water at the end of a treatment.

Avoid bright lights, especially directly over the mat or therapy bed. Move the mat/bed or lights, or use floor-standing or table lights instead. You can also use dimmer switches. Some people like to burn a candle because, as well as producing a nice soft glow, the candle flame "brings in the light," affirming that you are working in the light for the highest good.

CRYSTALS

Crystals for your therapy room can greatly enhance your treatments. This is so for any type of therapy or healing modality as well as Crystal Reiki Healing. When other people come into your healing space, they can have wonderful therapeutic experiences just from walking into the room. Remember to cleanse the crystals regularly, even the ones you have set in place permanently.

Amethyst

You will find the crystals most suited to you, but here is a quick tour of some of the crystals in my healing room to give you some examples of the crystals I find most suitable to work with:

Rose quartz

- **Amethyst:** I have two amethyst geodes in my healing room. One by the therapy bed to continually energize and cleanse it, and a second, which is programmed to cleanse other crystals, on my crystal table. It always gets an extra ting of the tingsha when I cleanse the room.

- **Rose quartz:** there is a large rose quartz under the therapy bed, approximately below where the heart of a client would be, to enhance the feeling of love. It's like giving a big, loving hug to whoever lies on the bed.

Black obsidian

- **Black obsidian:** this large crystal is kept underneath the feet end of the therapy bed to help with grounding.

- **Petrified wood:** a large piece on the floor absorbs stress as clients release it. There is always lots of anxiety and worry released during a treatment and petrified wood acts as a great sink for it, collecting it up and holding on to it so it can be cleared later when the room is cleansed.

Petrified wood

- **Lemurian quartz crystal:** kept on the floor by the window. it serves a few functions, such as bringing light and energy into the room and keeping the treatment focused.

Lemurian quartz crystal

Pyrite

Herkimer

Tourmaline

- **Pyrite:** there are several pyrite crystals along the windowsill to help reduce external distractions. Pyrite is particularly helpful for noisy neighbors! I have a golf club outside the window and these crystals help to reduce the noise down to the occasional thwack of a club against a golf ball.

- **Ruby, amethyst, and Herkimer diamond:** these are my special attunement crystals for Reiki initiations. However, I find them helpful in treatments, too, as every crystal experience can be an attunement to crystal energy at one level or another for both your client and you.

- **Tourmaline medicine wheel:** this protects the healing space and keeps it special (see page 56).

In addition, I have literally hundreds of crystals to work with in treatments, including a selection of master crystals and hematite for grounding when needed.

MULTIPURPOSE SPACES

Ideally you will have a dedicated room or space as a healing room. However, this is not always practical, so here are some suggestions that may help you if you have a multipurpose space. Firstly, clean and energetically cleanse the space. Consider using things like screens, throws, scarves, and pashminas to change the look of the room .Try to have a focus point you can easily create, such as a small table or stool with special crystals, a candle, or representations of the elements, planets, or points of the compass (see page 56). Plants, herbs, or flowers are also nice and bring color and aroma. Add a statue of any deity or angelic guardian you believe in. You can even add glitter and sparkles.

REVIEWING THE SPACE

When you have set up your room go outside, close the door, take three very deep breaths, re-enter the room, and see how it feels. Don't be afraid to change things now or as time goes by.

working with clients

There are very few right and wrongs regarding how to work with clients. First and foremost, always be yourself. People will be drawn to you because of your energy so be more you, rather than trying to be whatever you imagine a Crystal Reiki healer "should" be.

BE YOURSELF AND BE COMFORTABLE

If you are comfortable and relaxed, your client will be, too—don't worry about what you think they expect. Pay attention to personal hygiene as you will be working closely in people's auras. Tie back long hair so it doesn't fall on your client when you lean over them.

Your feet are also very important because as a Crystal Reiki healer you'll be standing most of the day. Consider if you want to work in shoes or barefoot. There are advantages and disadvantages to both. Working barefoot helps you connect to the ground and stay grounded. If you choose to work barefoot, as many healers do, make sure that your floor is vacuumed or swept and there are no crystal shards or anything else on the floor that might injure you or your client or cause discomfort.

BE PROFESSIONAL

You cannot make professional decisions if you are emotionally involved with a client. It's great to help your family and friends, but if they need to see a therapist for specific symptoms or issues regularly then they should see another unrelated professional. Similarly, if you believe there's someone better than you for this client, you feel out of your depth, or you just don't want to work with someone for any reason, refer them to someone else. You should never put yourself in a position you feel uncomfortable with a client.

Confidentiality is an absolute. Tell your client it is a confidential space. They will relax and be more open. With this in mind, I recommend asking them to fill in a client consent form, too[1].

BE PREPARED

Make sure your crystals are clean, cleansed, and arranged so you can select the appropriate ones quickly. The crystals you work with regularly can also be charged with Reiki (see page 38) so they are always ready to be used. If you are working as a mobile healer, or even if you have a multipurpose room at home, then the process of setting out your crystals prior to a treatment can help not only in creating a harmonious healing hot spot but also in making the space your own. You may find your crystals become a talking point as others observe you and are drawn into the energy you create around you. Whether you are working in a room, a tent, or even outside in a field, this will definitely help people to relax as they enter your special space. You will also feel empowered as you create your area for healing and make it distinct, which will enhance the success of every treatment you give.

Plan the order you are going to place crystals on your client. Going in one direction is better and less noticeable for your client than a haphazard approach. If you drop a crystal, leave it and work with another. If a crystal slips on a client, leave it—you can retrieve it later wherever it ends up! Assume it either wants to be where it has moved to (in which case it hasn't "slipped") or place another crystal where you think it needs to be.

Choose your setup, too—are you going to work on a therapy couch or pillows on the floor? When I started working as a crystal healer I always preferred working on the floor with lots of mats and pillows. Sometimes with Crystal Reiki Healing you will find that you are placing crystals around the body in the aura (see page 84) and this can be difficult on a therapy bed. If you do prefer a therapy bed, opt for a wider one rather than the "standard" 24-inch (60-cm) wide bed.

ARRANGING YOUR CRYSTALS

Whether you are working from a fixed location or traveling to different venues, many healers enjoy the gentle ritual of arranging their crystals before beginning a treatment as a way of focusing, centering, and grounding. You can arrange your crystals in the chakra/rainbow colors, in the shape of a compass (so north is always at the top or head of the bed), as a display in the shape of a heart, spiral, star, or animal, by mineral type, form, or size, aligned with the elements or planets, or any other way you feel works for you. There are no rules to this, only ideas as a starting point for your own creativity and requirements. Rituals can be as simple or complex as you need them to be.

TAKE CARE OF YOURSELF

Your treatment room should be able to hold all your client's issues, so they don't spill out into your life. Keeping all healing matters confidential is essential but it also helps in other ways. If your therapy room is a confidential space, and you make this clear to your clients, then it is easy for you to leave your client's problems in the room when you step out and close the door. If you find this difficult, then work with a crystal ball at the end of every working day. Once you've seen your last client and cleansed and tidied your therapy room, sit quietly with your crystal ball. Imagine in your mind a picture of your last client and watch as they float into the crystal ball, where the crystal will hold their energy and transmute it as it continues to send them healing. Do this with each client you have treated, one by one. (You can also do the same thing with anyone and anything else that is worrying you or causing you stress, such as the driver who cut you up on your way home or your mother-in-law who's visiting at the weekend.)

Psychic protection can help prevent you from taking on clients' "stuff"—their issues. Try wearing, or carrying in your pocket or bra, tourmaline or other protective crystals (see opposite) or create a tourmaline medicine wheel.

TOURMALINE MEDICINE WHEEL

The tourmaline medicine wheel gives protection in any situation or place where its energies are focused, and to anyone. Select one tourmaline crystal to represent you or your therapy room. Select eight others, so you have a total of nine tourmaline crystals. Place the crystal representing you on a table, the floor, or any flat surface and create a wheel around it, placing first the stone to the North, which represents the gods, or things that are out of your control. Then the West—the physical world, which usually relates to things like money, careers, and finance. Next, the South— everything that is nurturing, such as home and family. Before you place a crystal in the East, fill in the gaps—northeast, northwest, southwest, southeast—so that when you place the one in the East, which represents the gateway to the psychic and spiritual worlds, you are completing the circle and closing the wheel of protection.

PROTECTIVE CRYSTALS

Tourmaline—especially verdelite (green tourmaline),
rubellite (pink), and black tourmaline

Lapis lazuli

Ruby

Quartz

Red jasper

Mookaite

Tangerine quartz

Peridot

Kunzite

Angel aura quartz

Aqua aura

Aquamarine

Turquoise

Spirit quartz

Goddess stone

Obsidian

Pyrite

Agate

Stibnite

Smoky quartz

Red jasper

Kunzite

Pink rubellite

Aquamarine

Mookaite

preparing to begin healing

Make sure you have a calm space before you start so you can focus and center yourself. Many people benefit from some form of meditation, ritual or ceremony. Try holding your quartz master crystal (see page 21): look at the termination and ask your Crystal Reiki Guide, and any others who might help, to join you. If you have Reiki Level 2 or above, draw the Reiki symbols in the corners of the room. Then use the powering self-treatment exercise on page 68 or do the Crystal Reiki Healing Gassho meditation.

CRYSTAL REIKI HEALING GASSHO MEDITATION WITH QUARTZ MASTER CRYSTAL

Gassho means two hands coming together in the praying hand or prayer pose. It is a gesture used in the East for meditation and prayer as well as a sign of greeting, gratitude, reverence, or apology. It is also the only meditation we know that Usui Sensei practiced himself.

This is a perfect, simple meditation you can perform every day. It is suggested that you practice this for 20 minutes when you wake in the morning and before you go to bed at night. I recommend you start by doing at least 10 minutes daily and you will quickly see the positive results it can yield.

Sit down somewhere comfortably where you can keep your spine straight. Hold your quartz master crystal (see page 21) vertically, with the termination at the top, between your palms with your hands in prayer position in front of your chest. Focus your attention on the crystal tip. Try not to think about anything other than the tip of the crystal and allow yourself to relax. Thoughts will come into your mind. Don't get into a discussion or have an argument with them. Just accept them, let them pass through your mind, and bring your attention back to the tip of your crystal.

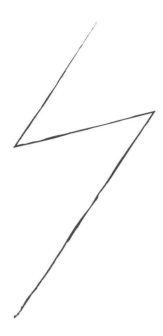

CRYSTAL REIKI GROUNDING

This is very simple but important. You should ensure you are grounded before you begin a treatment and that both you and anyone you are treating are grounded at the end. Some folks discover a floaty, airy feeling when either giving or receiving Crystal Reiki Healing and sometimes they really enjoy this experience. However, it is not helpful if you intend to do anything practical after the treatment—such as driving home!

To ground yourself, hold two hematite stones, one in each hand, recognizing their weight and imagining Reiki energy flowing from the top of your head all the way down your body to your feet. Take three deep breaths. Very quickly your hands will begin to feel heavy. This feeling grounds most people in a couple of minutes.

The Reiki symbol Raku (see page 34) can also be an excellent grounder. Try creating the raku symbol from hematite stones in your meditation room or under your therapy bed, if you have one. Simply having this symbol under the bed by the feet is grounding.

chapter 3
Crystal Reiki
treatments

This chapter explains the techniques needed to heal
yourself and others through Crystal Reiki treatments,
from a standard treatment working with the chakras
to crystal grids for specific purposes.

traditional Reiki hand positions

In the same way as there are conventional crystals that correlate to the chakras (see page 20), there are regular hand positions to carry out a Reiki treatment. These were designed to cover all the energy centers of the body. One of the joys about both Reiki and crystal healing is that the systems work by themselves. Both Reiki and crystals have a mind of their own and will help you direct healing energy to the areas it is most needed. This is not always where we think it might be. So when you start, it is always best to follow the traditional system. As you gain more experience, you open up possibilities of more intuitive treatments.

- For all positions, keep your fingers together and your hands flat or slightly cupped.

- When holding your hands in each position, you can either touch the body or hover your hands slightly above it.

- Similarly, if the position covers a crystal on the body, place your hands on or over the crystal.

- When treating others, you should always explain what you will be doing, where, and for how long, and, most importantly, obtain your client's consent for you to touch them.

- Each hand position should be held for 3–5 minutes.

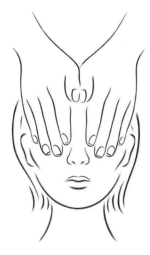

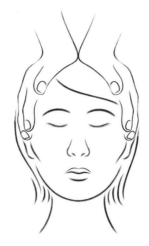

1. For the 1st position, begin at the top of the body: place your hands over the eyes.

2. For the 2nd position, place your hands on the crown of the head.

3. For the 3rd position, place your hands over the ears.

4. For the 4th position, place your hands on the back of the head or cranium.

5. For the 5th position, cup the chin.

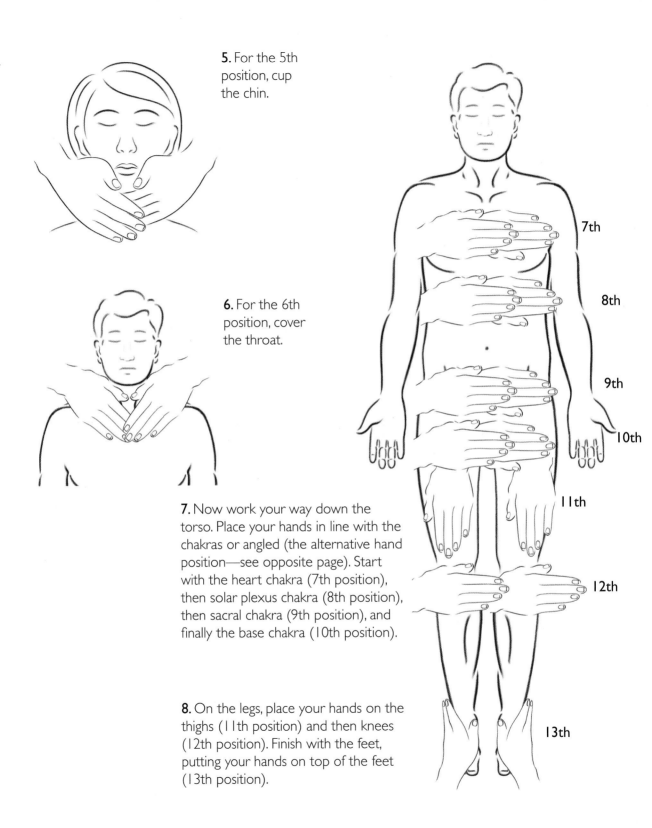

6. For the 6th position, cover the throat.

7th

8th

9th

10th

11th

12th

13th

7. Now work your way down the torso. Place your hands in line with the chakras or angled (the alternative hand position—see opposite page). Start with the heart chakra (7th position), then solar plexus chakra (8th position), then sacral chakra (9th position), and finally the base chakra (10th position).

8. On the legs, place your hands on the thighs (11th position) and then knees (12th position). Finish with the feet, putting your hands on top of the feet (13th position).

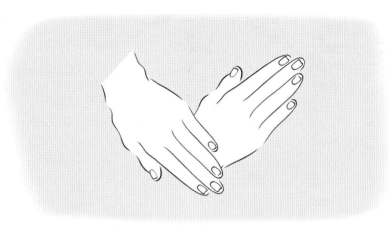

Alternative hand position

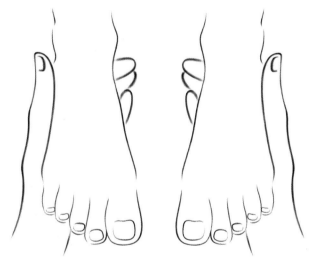

9. For the 14th position, hold each foot with both hands—it doesn't matter which foot you work with first.

10. Finally, hold the heels of both feet (15th position).

Crystal Reiki self-treatment

Crystal Reiki self-treatment can produce instant benefits: it creates relaxation, which relieves stress, pain, emotional upset, and physical injury. Regular self-treatment can help with many chronic conditions, such as irritable bowel syndrome (IBS) and arthritis. With all Crystal Reiki treatments, attunement to Reiki (see page 14) will enhance the experience.

1. Take your set of chakra crystals (see page 20) and cleanse them. Lie down and place the crystals on your chakras in the correct positions (see illustration). This is easiest if you start at the base chakra and add the crystals toward your crown so that you keep your head free for you to see what you are doing for longer. The crown chakra crystal is placed just above your head (see right). You will notice from the illustration that the chakras are not equidistant. The base and sacral chakras are close together, then there is a gap before the heart and solar plexus which form another pair, followed by another space, and finally the top three chakras—the crown, brow, and throat—are close together.

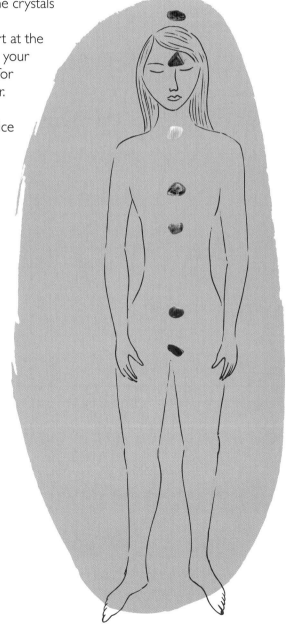

2. Once you have placed all the crystals, follow the Reiki self-treatment hand positions that are shown overleaf.

3. When you have completed the treatment, gently remove the crystals from your crown down—that is, in the reverse order you applied them. Some people like to curl up for a minute or two in the fetal position before they arise. Healing can be thirsty work so keep water available to drink (see box on page 50).

THE CROWN CHAKRA CRYSTAL

If you start to develop a headache during the treatment, move the crown chakra crystal closer to your head, and not further away as might seem to be the more obvious remedy. The headache here is caused by the crystal being placed above the crown chakra and its energy "pushing" down on the crown. By moving the crystal lower "into" the crown chakra, you remove the pressure and the headache disappears almost instantly.

SELF-TREATMENT HAND POSITIONS

The self-treatment hand positions are designed to cover all energy centers of the body (see page 19). Start at the head and gradually work down the body.

1. Begin by placing your hands over your eyes.

2. Next, place your hands on your temples.

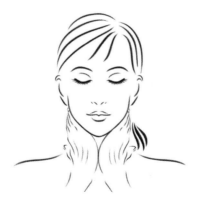

3. Place your hands on the back of your head or cranium.

4. Next, place your hands over your throat.

5. Now work your way down your torso. Position your hands across your body in line with the heart chakra.

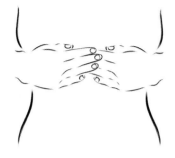 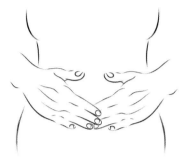 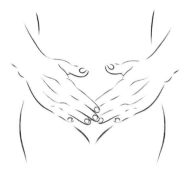

6. Next move your hands down to the solar plexus chakra.

7. Position your hands over the sacral chakra.

8. Finally, position your hands on the base chakra.

SIGNS AND SENSATIONS

As you work through each position you may simply become very relaxed or you may feel various sensations, such as tingling feelings and temperature changes, whether hot or cold. You might also become aware of emotions and physical irritations or discomfort. All these are signals that the treatment is working. Keep going and complete the treatment, and they will pass.

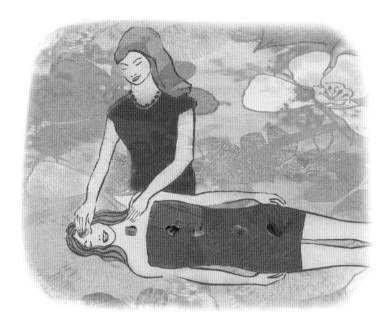

treating others with Crystal Reiki Healing

In the truest sense of the word, Crystal Reiki Healing is a *treat*-ment. Giving Reiki is considered a wonderful gift, crystal healing a beautiful sparkling practice. Add these together and you discover a cosmic healing experience.

CRYSTAL REIKI CHAKRA TREATMENT

With this standard practice you can treat any condition, because you select the crystals for whatever is being presented.

1. Firstly, ensure that you have all the crystals you may need to hand, and that you have set up and cleansed your room and crystals (see page 49). Take a moment to practice your Crystal Reiki Healing Gassho (see page 58) to bring your full focus and attention into the present. With your friend or client lying on your therapy bed or floor mat (there is no need for them to remove any clothing as both crystals and Reiki work through material), explain what you will be doing.

2. Next, start selecting the crystals you need. To begin with, choose one crystal for each chakra. When you start doing Crystal Reiki Healing treatments, it is probably best to work with the standard crystal chakra set (see page 20), but once you have a little experience, you can select crystals specifically for each person you treat. You can do this intuitively, with your pendulum, or with Reiki (see pages 42–47). Place these crystals on the appropriate chakras (see page 19).

3. Commence by placing your hands over the crystal at the crown, then work down the body following the Reiki hand positions (see pages 62–65). Remove the brow crystal when you Reiki the cranium (4th position) and replace it after this hand position is completed. In a traditional Reiki treatment, the client is turned onto their front and similar hand positions are repeated on their back. Because in a Crystal Reiki Healing treatment crystals are placed on the body as well as Reiki being channeled through the practitioner's hands, it is neither necessary nor practical to turn the client during the treatment.

4. When you have completed all the hand positions, it is nice to leave your friend or client for 5–10 minutes with the crystals still on them so they can experience a crystal energy bath. It creates a beautiful relaxing sensation. At the end of the treatment, remove the crystals, brush down and seal the aura with a Reiki charged selenite aura wand (see page 75).

A selenite aura wand

ADDITIONAL CRYSTAL REIKI HEALING TECHNIQUES

The following techniques can be applied as part of the standard treatment for more specific healing requirements.

PLACING CRYSTALS IN SOMEONE'S HANDS

Charge two hand-sized crystals with Reiki (see page 38) and place one in each of your client's hands. I find quartz crystals are good for physical healing, rose quartz for emotional challenges, green calcite for anxiety or panic attacks, and hematite for grounding. However, don't be afraid to go with your intuition, which you can always check with your pendulum (see page 42).

PLACING CRYSTALS DIRECTLY ON THE AFFECTED AREA

Dowse crystals with your pendulum for a specific complaint, such as an injured knee or troublesome bowel (for example, ask your pendulum, "Will this crystal help to heal my client's injured knee?"), and add them to the area concerned. You can also select specific crystals from the Crystal Finder in Chapter 5. You can Reiki these crystals by placing your hands over them and letting Reiki flow and, if you are attuned to Reiki Level 2 or above, focusing on appropriate symbols while the crystals are on the body.

RELEASING ENERGY BLOCKS

Our chakras go in and out of balance completely naturally throughout the day. Balancing your chakras with a Crystal Reiki self-treatment daily (see page 68) can help to keep you healthy. However sometimes things happen, such as infections, injuries, emotional upsets, and traumatic encounters, and we find that one or more chakras won't come back into balance easily. This is often the case when a client comes to me because they have not been doing a regular self-healing regime and have developed symptoms they are now presenting. Frequently, this is because they have developed a "block" somewhere in their energy system. I've put block in "speech marks" because it is unlikely to be a total blockage of energy—that would lead to a very serious health condition—but more likely a partial blockage. To treat this, we add four mini quartz crystals in the shape of a star or cross around the relevant chakra.

Releasing long-term blocks can have dramatic healing and life-changing effects. Some people will find letting go of their long-term blocks challenging, as often they created the blocks themselves for very good reasons at the time. These might have worked to protect them emotionally and may have served a useful function. For example, I had a client whose mother was not demonstrative and showed no outward signs of affection when she was a child. In fact, every time she approached her mother for a hug, she was rejected. She very soon learned not to go to her mother for physical affection. Matter resolved—no more rejection. However, this created an energy block in her heart chakra. As time went by, this block that she had put up herself started to affect her life and she had difficulty forming meaningful

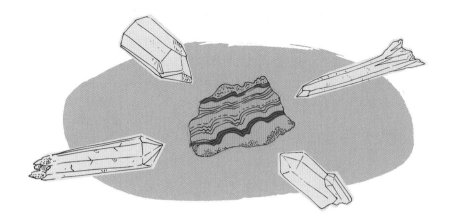

relationships because she'd taught herself not to permit the opportunity for rejection to exist. Although very challenging and emotional, releasing this block was life-changing in the most positive way for her.

After placing the chakra crystals, ask your pendulum if there is a "block" over each chakra in turn. Wherever you receive a positive response, add four mini quartz crystals with their terminations pointing in toward the chakra crystal. When you Reiki a "blocked" chakra, spend a little more time on it to check the block has dissolved. You might feel this in your hands, see a change in the client's breathing, notice muscle twitches, or generally sense the release of energy. If you have difficulty feeling this, you can always ask your pendulum after treating the chakra with Reiki for a few minutes.

IMPROVING REIKI FLOW

The minor chakras in the palms of your hands, where Reiki flows from you to your client, can be super activated with a quartz crystal before giving a Reiki treatment. To do this, simply hold the crystal in your right hand with the termination pointing toward the palm of your left hand, about an inch (2–3 cm) away from it. Move the crystal slowly in clockwise circles for 2–3 minutes and you will begin to feel a sensation in the palm of your left hand. People describe this feeling differently but often as a pulling, heating, or tingling in the palm. Then change hands and repeat the process to activate the chakra in your right hand.

ENDING TREATMENTS

I always prefer to finish any treatment by combing and sealing the aura, because it rounds off the treatment nicely and leaves friends and clients feeling snug and secure. During the treatment, energy is released through the client's chakras. Some of it will clear by itself, but some will remain dangling in their aura. To remove this unhelpful energy, it is recommended to comb the aura with selenite, and a selenite aura wand is best for this purpose as it glides through the aura and enhances your sensations of the energy. Before you start your treatment, remember to Reiki your selenite aura wand alongside all your other crystals (see page 38), so it is ready to perform at the end of the treatment.

COMBING THE AURA

After you have removed all the crystals from your client, starting at the head, gently pass the selenite aura wand through their aura 2–3 inches (5–8 cm) above the body, as if you are combing through long hair, with the intent of brushing out any unhelpful energy that's tapped there. Do this very slowly and you will see how the selenite amplifies the energy in the aura so you can feel and notice any sticky areas or knots as you comb through it. These sticky areas may feel as if they're hot or cool, gloopy or uncomfortable, or even a tiny electric shock. The slower you go, the more you will feel. Clients often say this is very comforting; it's like a very gentle release of something they can't quite identify, but they feel better for letting it go.

Work with a selenite aura wand to comb the aura.

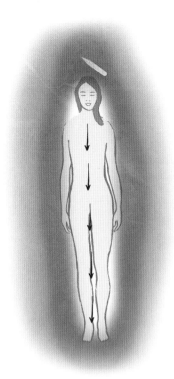
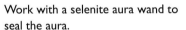

Work with a selenite aura wand to seal the aura.

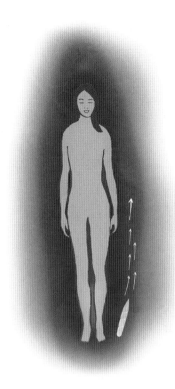

Work with the wand to send any unwanted energy away.

SEALING THE AURA

The final step is to seal the aura with your selenite aura wand. This prolongs the treatment for the client and allows for ongoing healing after leaving you. Simply hold the selenite aura wand horizontally and pointing away from you, a couple of inches (5 cm) above your client's crown chakra, and move it evenly through the aura along the central meridian line all the way down to the feet. Your intention should be for the wand to collect any unhealthy energy still lurking in the aura. Then, from the feet, move it back to the crown, stretching up as high as you can to expand the aura to the maximum possible size, then bring the wand down above the crown chakra again. Finally, move the wand straight down to the feet again. From there, direct the wand toward a window to send any unwanted energy straight out of it; if there is no window, point the wand toward a crystal ball instead, but remember to cleanse the ball afterward.

Crystal Reiki grids

Now you have mastered the basic techniques of a Crystal Reiki Healing treatment, we can look at some more advanced methods. Here we build crystal grids on or around the body to magnify the Crystal Reiki Healing.

With all of the following treatments you should firstly prepare your healing room and yourself as explained in Chapter 2. Pay particular attention to cleansing your sacred Crystal Reiki Healing space and the crystals you will be working with. Do your Crystal Reiki protection and grounding exercises and place any crystals in the Reiki environment that you might need. Take a moment to breathe and center yourself by holding your quartz master crystal in the Crystal Reiki Healing Gassho position while imagining the violet ray of Reiki flowing into your heart chakra and slowly filling your whole body. Call in your crystal and Reiki guides to join you (see page 21).

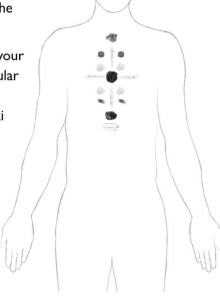

HEART AND EMOTIONS

This treatment places a crystal grid over the heart chakra to create a super-charged Crystal Reiki Healing treatment suitable for any emotional distress, heartbreak, or grief and can help to break emotional patterns set in the past, from your childhood or youth. As well as easing any physical heart and lung complaints, this treatment opens the heart chakra, which helps us to forgive, promotes a sense of freedom, and helps to relieve physical symptoms of stress, bringing relaxation. It can help you to "walk your talk"—to be yourself and communicate and act "from the heart," which in turn brings the opportunity for true loving relationships.

1. Start building the crystal grid in the center of the body by placing the ruby on the heart chakra in the middle of the chest. Then place the four mini quartz points around it with the terminations pointing in toward the ruby as shown. Pop a rose quartz in between each pair of quartz points.

2. Add the turquoise, pair of malachite crystals, and rhodochrosite as shown, and then the pairs of tourmaline and smoky quartz crystals. As you create this Crystal Reiki grid in this order, you will see it start to unfold before you.

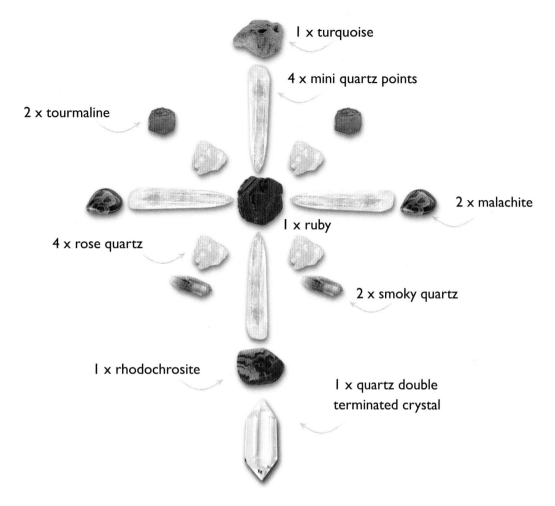

1 x turquoise

4 x mini quartz points

2 x tourmaline

2 x malachite

1 x ruby

4 x rose quartz

2 x smoky quartz

1 x rhodochrosite

1 x quartz double terminated crystal

3. Finally, place the double-terminated quartz crystal in position. If you wish, you may also place two hematite stones by the client's feet to keep them grounded (see page 145).

4. Place your hands in the first position and work down the body through each of the hand positions (see pages 62–65), spending three minutes or so in each position. If you place your hands on the body rather than over, do so carefully so as not to disturb the crystals.

5. At the end of the treatment, gently remove the crystals and put them into a suitable receptacle for cleansing, such as a wicker basket or soft-lined bowl. Then comb and seal the aura with your selenite aura wand (see page 74).

6. Thank your crystal and Reiki guides, then let your client know you have finished their treatment and that they may arise slowly. It is always nice to offer your client some Crystal Reiki water (see page 50) as they can often become thirsty—and remember to keep yourself hydrated, too, if you have a day of healing clients ahead of you! If you can, allow a little time at the end of the treatment for your client to talk about their experience if they wish.

PHYSICAL BOOST

This grid focuses on the solar plexus. It brings a boost of physical and emotional energy and inner strength in trying times. Specific benefits include speeding all physical healing of injuries and internal repair to damaged or worn tissues in chronic conditions, such as arthritis, COPD, and long-term digestive disorders (for example, Crohn's disease and colitis). It can also be helpful for chronic pain relief.

1. Begin building the grid by placing the center citrine crystal on the solar plexus. Then add the other four citrine crystals and four mini quartz points around it.

2. Put the rhodochrosite in place just below the heart with the two imperial topaz crystals alongside and the double-terminated quartz crystal vertically above.

3. Finally, add the peridot crystal below with the two amber stones on either side of it. If you wish, you may also place two hematite stones by the client's feet to keep them grounded (see page 145).

4. Follow steps 4–6 on pages 63–64 to proceed through the hand positions, remove the crystals, comb and seal the aura, and thank your guides.

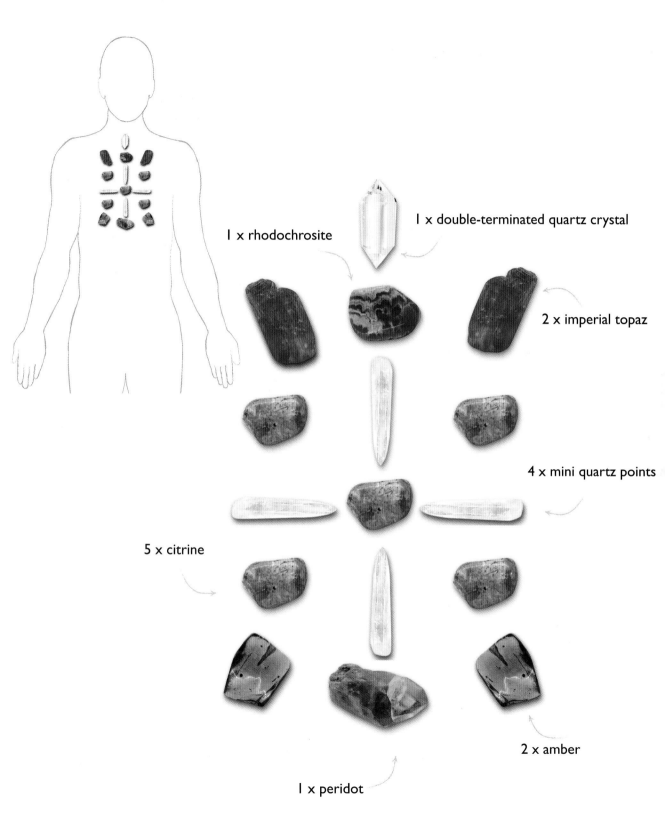

1 x rhodochrosite

1 x double-terminated quartz crystal

2 x imperial topaz

4 x mini quartz points

5 x citrine

2 x amber

1 x peridot

RELAXATION

Building a crystal grid across the whole body takes a little patience, but it becomes much easier after you've practiced it a few times. This layout is designed to bring your client relief from the stresses and strains of their everyday life. It allows them to let go of their worries and concerns and just to be in a place of complete deep relaxation. This really is a *treat*-ment! It is very good for any stressful situation and conditions exacerbated by stress—for example, skin conditions, such as psoriasis and eczema, and digestive disorders, such as irritable bowel syndrome—as well as emotional disorders, such as social phobias and depression.

1. Place a green calcite crystal in each of your client's hands.

2. Continue placing the layout, starting with the amethyst cluster at the crown and working down the body. Place the lapis lazuli on the center of the forehead and then very carefully add four mini quartz points around it, with their terminations pointing away from the lapis lazuli. Be careful not to let them roll or slip as you place them, as you are particularly near the eyes.

3. Place the turquoise on the throat with the four mini quartz points around it, with their terminations pointing away. The two blue lace agate crystals should be placed below but quite close to the turquoise, with a mini quartz point between them pointing straight down the center of the body.

4. Now build the grid around the heart chakra. This is a beautiful part of the layout, so pause for a moment and check in with your Crystal Reiki guides, asking them to guide you (see page 21). Place one rose quartz stone in the center of the chest. Place the four mini quartz points as shown, with their terminations pointing in toward this central rose quartz. In between these, place the four aventurine stones and pop another rose quartz at the end of each mini quartz point. Take a moment to appreciate the beauty here…

5. Next, put the orange calcite with four mini quartz points pointing in toward it on the solar plexus chakra, and chrysocolla on the sacral chakra with four quartz mini points around it in the same fashion. Add the citrine crystal between them. Place the peridot and tourmaline either side of the sacral chakra arrangement, and finish by putting the red tiger's eye and red calcite on the base chakra.

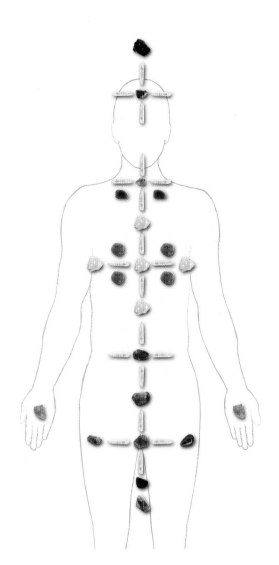

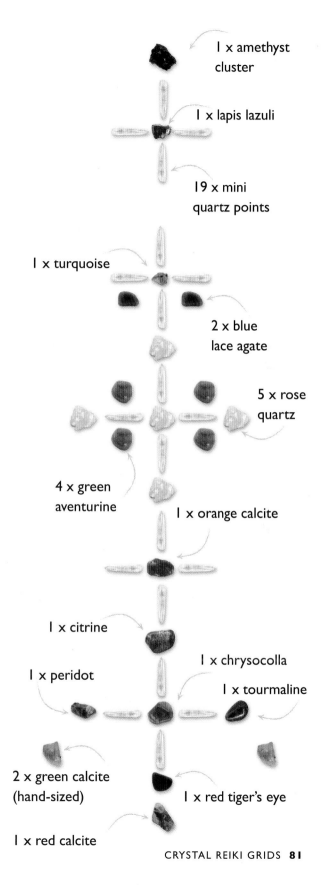

1 x amethyst cluster

1 x lapis lazuli

19 x mini quartz points

1 x turquoise

2 x blue lace agate

5 x rose quartz

4 x green aventurine

1 x orange calcite

1 x citrine

1 x chrysocolla

1 x peridot

1 x tourmaline

2 x green calcite (hand-sized)

1 x red tiger's eye

1 x red calcite

6. Follow steps 4–6 on pages 63–64 to proceed through the hand positions, remove the crystals, comb and seal the aura, and thank your guides. Be aware that your client might be extremely relaxed from this treatment, so allow some extra time so that you don't need to rush them out at the end. Give them hematite to ground them if necessary.

SPIRITUAL AWARENESS

This layout is designed to send energy up through your client's energy system to help them connect to the Reiki source. It makes the client more aware of energies within their body, as well as energetic exchanges between people, psychic phenomenon, and spiritual connections. It can assist with many conditions rooted in the psyche, such as listlessness and confusion, as well as helping the recipient to find direction in life and discover answers to their questions. The layout runs up the median line of the body, as straight as is practical.

This treatment usually produces an exhilarating feeling for both client and Crystal Reiki healer. The effects are often subtle and may be noticed over the two to three weeks that follow. During this time, it is not unusual for some clients to develop minor physical symptoms, such as a cold or upset tummy, as a deeper awareness of their own spirituality develops. As the Reiki is directed through the crystals, it subtly shifts and challenges your understanding of your world and sometimes our bodies react a little. It's nothing to be worried about and will pass quickly as your energy settles and inner comprehension deepens.

1. Start placing stones from the base chakra up, with the pyrite, amber, citrine, ruby, kyanite, sapphire, and amethyst cluster in order on the seven major chakras. Then place the imperial topaz next to the citrine and the blue topaz below the kyanite.

2. Begin from the base again and fill the gaps with mini quartz points, with all the terminations directed towards the crown. If possible, try to have each of the crystals touching each other so there are no gaps in the line.

3. For this treatment, work through the hand positions (see pages 62–65) in reverse. Start by placing your hands in the last position (15th) and work backward from the feet up the body. It may not be practical to use the cranium hand position (4th) if the crystals across the face and head are likely to slip out of place

4. Follow steps 5–6 on page 77 to remove the crystals, comb and seal the aura, and thank your guides.

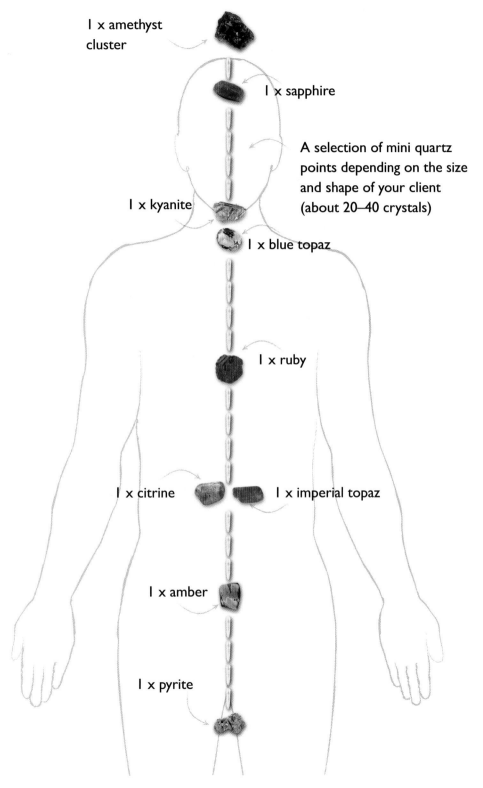

1 x amethyst cluster

1 x sapphire

A selection of mini quartz points depending on the size and shape of your client (about 20–40 crystals)

1 x kyanite

1 x blue topaz

1 x ruby

1 x citrine

1 x imperial topaz

1 x amber

1 x pyrite

HEALING THE AURA

We interact with everyone and everything through our aura. When your aura is strong and healthy, you can interact with people without feeling tired and drained. When it is run-down, you start to feel the effects of what seems like everyone else's energy on you. Your aura protects you and filters your experience with the outside world. When your aura is robust, it helps to protect you from bugs and colds, you retain emotional stability in trying times, and you are more focused in all you do. This treatment boosts confidence; it is subtle, and often, after a few days, people discover they are empowered to do simple things they would not previously have attempted.

In this treatment, crystals are placed in a specific order around the person, rather than on the body, forming a crystal "egg" around them. You can set this up before they arrive if you wish, so they simply lie down in the crystal egg when they arrive. If treating several clients, you can leave this layout set up and treat one person after another, as long as you cleanse the crystals and space before each treatment. It is best to work on the floor rather than a therapy bed for this treatment so that you are not limited by space.

Note that in the diagram the chakras are included as a guide to where the crystals are positioned around the body. So, for example, the two ruby crystals are in line with the heart, and the two sugilite crystals are in line with the brow.

1. Start by placing the amethyst above the crown chakra, the two celestite crystals either side of the crown, and the two sugilite crystals either side of the brow chakra. Two of the labradorite stones are placed either side of the throat chakra, then the rubies by the heart, citrine by the solar plexus, tourmaline by the sacral chakra, and rutilated quartz crystals either side of the base chakra. Place two of the clear quartz stones by the knees, two by the feet, and two by the heels inside the oval being created by the crystals. Now add the four remaining labradorite crystals: one above the amethyst at the crown, one outside the ruby to the right of the heart, one outside the citrine to the left of the solar plexus, and the final one at the bottom of the oval centrally beneath the feet. Lastly, place one clear quartz point pointing away from the head above the amethyst and labradorite at the crown.

2. Add the quartz points to complete the crystal egg. If you have enough quartz points, complete the egg with all the crystals touching, but if you don't have enough, simply try to keep the crystals evenly spread out and make sure there is at least one quartz crystal between any other types of crystal—except at the crown (celestite) and brow (sugilite), where there isn't usually physically enough room to do this. The number of quartz crystals needed will vary depending on the height of the person receiving the treatment.

3. Follow steps 4–6 on pages 63–64 to proceed through the hand positions, remove the crystals, comb and seal the aura, and thank your guides.

Many clear quartz points (at least 19; see step 2)—these can be mini points or larger crystals

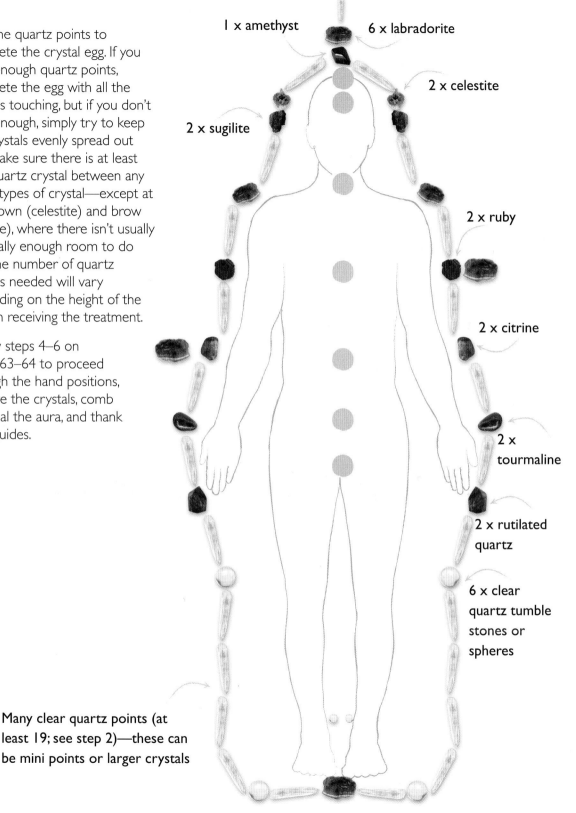

1 x amethyst

6 x labradorite

2 x celestite

2 x sugilite

2 x ruby

2 x citrine

2 x tourmaline

2 x rutilated quartz

6 x clear quartz tumble stones or spheres

chapter 4

enhance YOUR world WITH Crystal Reiki

Make your home a beautiful Reiki environment and discover other ways to work with Crystal Reiki, such as distant healing, calming tension, and healing animals and plants.

Crystal Reiki in the home

Crystals alter the energies in their surroundings. They magnify Reiki and they affect everything around them. Have you noticed the feeling when you bring a new crystal home, step into a crystal store, or visit a friend who has lots of crystals? They can influence the atmosphere in your living room, office, kitchen, bathroom, and bedroom, as well as your therapy room (see page 48). You can bring crystals into every space in your world.

You can change or focus the energy in any room for any purpose. For example, you may want to make your therapy room calm and relaxing or your dining room convivial and socially interactive. When you have decided what you want each room or area to do, and how you want it to feel, select some crystals. You can consult the Crystal Finder (see page 105) for ideas, ask your pendulum to help (see page 42), or simply opt for crystals you're drawn to—I believe that crystals choose you, too! When you've chosen your crystals, Reiki each one for a few minutes (see page 38). This helps the crystals tune into the Reiki energy ray and perform even better.

To direct the energy of these crystals, bring in some quartz crystal points and place them around the edge of the room all facing the same way, either into the room or out toward the walls. When they're pointing in, they will give the room an energy boost—good for encouraging focus. Point them toward the walls and they will help to ease energy out—great at the end of the day when you want to wind down and relax. Try this around your bath: add a rose quartz rough rock into the water—carefully, so you don't scratch the bath—and light a candle and some incense, then give yourself a Crystal Reiki self-treatment for a complete de-stressing wind-down.

ROOM BY ROOM

Whatever the size of your home, or purpose of your space, crystals can enhance the feeling. They bring natural beauty into your environment. Add some Reiki to your crystals and watch them change your world. Crystals can improve specific zones within a single room, so even if you have a studio

| Carnelian | Green moss agate | Obsidian | Jet | Citrine |

apartment you can follow this advice to place different crystals according to their purpose—for example, bringing calm in an area for relaxation to one part and encouraging focus in another area for work or study. You can also Reiki any room by visualizing the symbols and drawing them (whether literally or in the air) around the room. Hanging Reiki artwork and imagery also taps into the powerful energy. Below are a few suggestions to open your eyes to a home of Crystal Reiki possibilities.

KITCHEN

- To help you focus on recipes, place carnelian and pyrite in the kitchen.

- Citrine and tourmaline encourage creativity which can help you be more inventive in your cooking.

- Carnelian, muscovite, fulgurite, grey banded or green moss agate, pyrite, obsidian, jet, violet flame opal, lepidolite, tourmaline, labradorite, chrysocolla, peridot, yellow jasper, tiger's eye and citrine are all helpful in the kitchen and are good for digestion, too.

- If you ever feel a bit spacey while cooking, obsidian and jet are grounding .

- Reiki your food by placing your hands over the food on your plate and letting that Reiki energy flow. You can also Reiki your pots, pans, and dishes as you are cooking. (If you find yourself in a place where you're not sure about the quality of the food, always Reiki it before eating and carry citrine, which really helps to prevent and ease cases of nausea and food poisoning.)

DINING ROOM

- Place crystals around the room to aid digestion (see the kitchen suggestions above).

- Add some relaxing amethyst, calming calcite, and some blue lace agate or kyanite to help the conversation flow.

- A crystal centerpiece in the middle of a formal dining table looks amazing and brings the focus, energetically and aesthetically, to the food.

- Reiki the room before guests arrive by drawing the Reiki symbols around the room.

LIVING ROOM

Living rooms serve many functions so here be as personal as you like with your choice of crystals. Think of what you do in your living room and how you would like to feel there and select crystals accordingly. Be intuitive, check the Crystal Finder (see page 105) and ask your pendulum (see page 42) if you're in doubt. The following suggestions are what I have in my own living room: I keep about sixty crystals there, all with different intentions.

- An amethyst geode brings calm and continually refreshes the energy.

- A Himalayan salt lamp produces negative ions to keep the room fresh.

- Celestite connects to dreams, and flint in the form of prehistoric tools helps you remember and connect to ancestors.

- For protection, keep pyrite on the windowsill and a tourmaline medicine wheel (I have one by the window that was once broken in through).

- For connection to spirit, I have a tanzanite Buddha, quartz Buddha, and a meteorite.

- A large tourmalinated citrine crystal brings joy and happiness.

- A Lemurian quartz crystal is my home master crystal, as I keep my working crystals in my healing room at my showroom and it's always good to keep one handy.

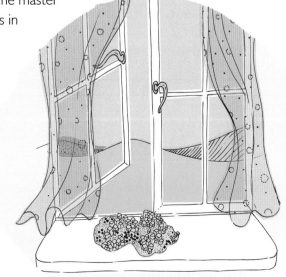

- Crystals with a purpose or memory attached are another great addition. One special crystal friend in my living room is the quartz crystal used as the model for the cover of my very first meditation album.

BEDROOM

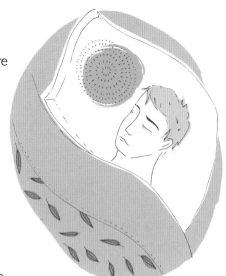

- Malachite is my go-to crystal for sleep patterns. If you're having disturbed nocturnal patterns, hold a malachite stone for an hour or so before you want to go to sleep. Just carry on with whatever you're doing and take it to bed beside you, either under your pillow or on your nightstand. This works very quickly for some people, but everyone sees an improvement in their sleep patterns over a couple of weeks.

- Celestite and lapis lazuli are good for dreams and dream recall.

- Ruby protects you from nightmares and you could also hang a dreamcatcher over your bed for this.

- Mookaite, moldavite, jade, and spirit quartz can all help dreams and a pleasant night's sleep.

- Red jasper at the foot of the bed is grounding and helps channel away the worries of the day.

- Tourmaline is protective and clears worries from the head and heart.

- Rhodochrosite is a passion stone that is capable of lighting a spark in a tepid relationship.

- Falcon's eye can help someone express their sexuality.

HOME OFFICE

- Place quartz crystals around the room pointing in toward the center to help you focus.

- Keep fluorite, snow quartz, and citrine on your desk for clarity and inspiration.

- Place your hands on your keyboard or notepad at the start of the day and fill them up with positive Reiki vibes.

crystals and Reiki in your environment

Some of the effects crystals can have as a result of being around you include holding emotions and thoughts, both happy ones you wish to share and disharmonious ones you want to remove. In the former case, fill a crystal with love and Reiki (see page 38) and let that dissipate out of the crystal during the day; it'll be an energy freshener—just like an air freshener, but for energy. Harmonizing energy helps healing, hastening recovery. Crystals provide protection, creating safe and secure sensations for everyone, including visitors. They can energize and calm emotions, bring healing, cleanse, and maintain clarity. They can also be very helpful by someone's bed when they're unwell or in hospital.

CRYSTAL REIKI HEALING BALL FOR CALMING RIVALRIES

There are situations where there may be discordant energy, resulting in disagreements, arguments, and bad feeling. This can be any situation where rivals are in the same place, such as at work, with competing teams, sports, lovers, family, friends, and siblings. There is a magical Crystal Reiki Healing remedy! You will need a quartz crystal ball.

1. Hold the quartz crystal ball in both hands and let Reiki flow into it (see page 55). If you have Reiki Level 2, visualize the Reiki symbols floating inside the sphere, one at a time. Hon Sha Ze Sho Nen is particularly helpful as it transcends time and space: rivalries are often reactions to acts that have happened already—that is, acts in the past.

2. Place the crystal ball in the area where malcontent is being expressed. At the end of every day, remove the crystal ball and thoroughly cleanse it under running water before replacing it. Keep doing this for two or three weeks and you will notice the arguments and divisions reduce until they completely stop.

distant healing

Sometime around the summer of 1994, I was quietly sitting in the garden doing a drumming meditation. (OK, not *that* quietly!) I had surrounded myself with crystals, called in my guides, and let Reiki flow through the drumstick. It was mid-afternoon on a bright summer's day when I started. I stopped after what I believed was twenty or thirty minutes and opened my eyes in darkness. It was 11.30pm. Losing track of time had transcended me to another place, an alternative reality; when I came back, as well as being a little surprised, I had a clear realization: if we all spent just a few minutes each day sending out healing to the planet, to those we love, those we know, those we dislike, and even those we don't know at all, whether two-legged, four-legged, winged, finned, Standing People (the sacred Native American term for trees) or Stone People, or spirit… whatever and whoever, we could change the world. It's not an original idea and it's a bit hippie, but it is absolutely true!

It is my belief that whatever your experience with Crystal Reiki Healing, whether you are a novice or Crystal or Reiki Master teacher, we can all do this, and indeed should. Sending out positive thoughts on the Reiki ray and empowered with crystals not only helps others and the planet, it does you good, too! Although it is not why you do it, you benefit from the positivity flowing through your energy system and out through your aura.

Crystals are valuable companions for sending distant healing (also known as absent healing) because they focus and store energy and can be programmed to help with the task at hand. They also contribute their own energy to the healing experience. There are many ways of sending distant healing, from simply focusing your thoughts on someone who could do with a little extra energy to elaborate ceremonies and intricate crystal grids. However, you choose to send distant healing, make certain that you do it. Try it right now.

SENDING DISTANT HEALING WITH CRYSTAL REIKI

Take hold of your quartz master crystal, focus your mind on who or where you are sending healing, and say to yourself "Reiki on!". If you are attuned to Reiki Level 2 or higher, then you can also visualize Hon Sha Ze Sho Nen or draw it with your crystal. Feel the energy stream through you and out through your quartz master crystal. Keep this thought going for five minutes, or ten, or half an hour or an hour if you have the time. But even if you have only two minutes—do it!

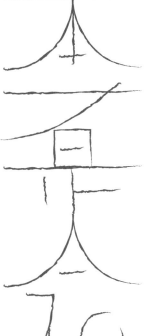

The best way to carry out distant healing is to make it part of your everyday ritual, just like a shower or brushing your teeth. You can select certain crystals to help with specific types of healing, which you can use alongside or instead of your quartz master crystal. For example, you could choose one crystal just to help people with physical problems, another for emotional issues, and a third for mental unrest, or you could select one for people, another for animals, one for plants, and one more for the planet. (For other methods of distant healing, see page 31.)

USING A HEALING BOOK

One of the ways I like to send distant healing is through a healing book. I simply write the names of people who need healing in the book. When I send healing, I draw the symbols over the book with my master crystal and then hold the book between my hands until I feel the heat of the Reiki flowing through the book. I keep this flowing for a few minutes. Then finally I place my distant healing crystal ball on its stand upon the book and leave it to keep sending healing to everyone in the book until I revisit it the next day.

Crystal Reiki grids to empower your life

Rather than placing your crystals randomly, you can place them in a specific pattern known as a crystal grid. Your crystals work as a team, creating the capacity for energy to produce transformation, healing, and manifestation. When you add Reiki, the possibilities and power are magnified.

Before creating these grids, find a time and place you won't be disturbed, put up a "do not disturb" sign (whether physical or metaphorical), and turn off your phone, because it is important you maintain focus during the grid creation process. A Crystal Reiki Healing grid does not need to physically be in the space it is working in, so you can set these up in your healing room where they won't be disturbed.

With all these grids, the first step is to cleanse your crystals (see page 49) and then to Reiki each crystal until they are all overflowing with this energy.

GRID FOR PROBLEM-SOLVING

It's not only people, animals, the Earth, and other tangible "things" that you can direct Crystal Reiki Healing toward, but also to ideas and concepts, problems and challenges, and other situations. The triangle is the strongest shape in nature and the solidity of the Crystal Reiki triangle grid helps you see the answers you need to find. Whatever the problem is, it can be looked at as a triangle of events. One point is where you currently stand, the second is the issue that concerns you, and the third is the solution. It is best if you avoid being attached to a particular outcome; let things just happen as they should, rather than holding on to a desire, as there might be a much better outcome that you cannot imagine right now.

1. Trace or copy the triangle from page 151 to create a paper grid. On the paper grid, write your name over the bottom right corner of the triangle, a description of the issue on the bottom left corner, and "solution for the highest good" on the top corner.

2. Place the quartz crystal cluster in the center of the triangle. Then put the ruby crystal over your name on the bottom right corner, the obsidian over the problem or issue on the bottom left corner, and the amethyst at the top point of the triangle to represent the solution. Place a mini quartz point in between each of the crystals. These should point from the ruby to obsidian, from obsidian to amethyst and amethyst to ruby.

3. With your hand, draw each of the Reiki symbols in the air over the grid, then place your hands palm facing down just above it and allow Reiki to flow through the whole grid for 5–10 minutes. Leave the grid where it won't be disturbed.

4. Once the issue has been resolved, you can dismantle the Crystal Reiki Healing grid, cleanse the crystals so they are ready for their next mission, and destroy the paper grid, sending its energy either to the universe by burning it in a fireproof receptacle or to the earth by shredding it and adding it to your compost or recycling.

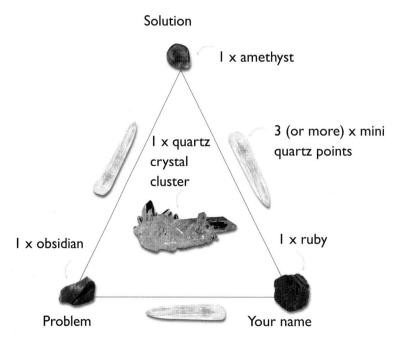

Solution

1 x amethyst

3 (or more) x mini quartz points

1 x quartz crystal cluster

1 x obsidian

1 x ruby

Problem

Your name

GRID FOR HEALING

This is another excellent way to send distant healing (see page 93) to anyone, whether you know them or not, disaster areas, and the planet. For this we are using the spiral shape, which represents the universal spiral of healing energy.

1. Trace or copy the spiral from page 152 to create a paper grid. Place the quartz crystal ball in the center of the spiral; this will keep sending healing well after you have stopped. Next, create the spiral path with the amethyst crystals from the quartz crystal ball out to the end of the spiral. Place the ruby at the end to represent your healing spark.

2. With your hand, draw each of the Reiki symbols in the air over the grid, then place your hands palm facing down just above it and allow Reiki to flow through the whole grid for 5–10 minutes. Imagine you are sending Reiki from the ruby along the amethyst path, as if the ruby is sparking the amethyst fuse of Crystal Reiki Healing energy. When it reaches the crystal ball, it flows out to whoever or wherever it is being directed. When you stop sending Reiki into the grid, leave the crystal layout intact and the quartz crystal ball will continue to send Crystal Reiki Healing.

Approx. 20 x amethyst

3. If you've set this up for one person or event, once the grid's task is completed, you can dismantle the Crystal Reiki Healing grid, cleanse the crystals so they are ready for their next mission, and destroy the paper grid, sending its energy either to the universe by burning it in a fireproof receptacle or to the earth by shredding it and adding it to your compost or recycling. However, if you want to send general healing energy toward the planet, you can leave the grid in place and recharge it with Reiki monthly on the new moon.

1 x ruby

1 x quartz crystal ball

CRYSTAL REIKI HEALING GRID FOR LOVE AND RELATIONSHIPS

Everyone needs somebody; everybody needs love. Whether that's a new relationship, enhancing or re-energizing a current one, or strengthening a friendship or family tie, this grid will help. We use the Flower of Life grid as the base because, just like any healthy relationship, it has multiple layers that intertwine.

1. Trace or copy the template from page 153 to create a paper grid. Place the ruby on the flower in the center of the grid. Next add the six quartz crystals on the petals of this central flower with the terminations pointing in toward the ruby and the six rose quartz around it on the flowers neighboring it. Then place the twelve amethysts on the flowers in the next row and finally the remaining crystals on the outermost flowers and linking points in this order: emerald starting on the eastern flower (furthest right) and placing in a clockwise direction from here morganite, malachite, eudialyte, aventurine, kunzite, clinochlore, rhodochrosite, and chrysocolla and then repeat the same order around the rest of the flower of life.

2. Now take your quartz master crystal and visualize it filled with lots of Sei He Ki symbols. Imagine Reiki and love flowing into the crystal until it's almost ready to explode with Reiki and love. Then with the quartz master crystal draw a big Sei He Ki over the whole grid and then a smaller one over the ruby crystal in the center. Then working clockwise from the emerald in the eastern position draw a Sei He Ki over each of the crystals in the outer circle, then the amethysts, the rose quartz, and finally the six quartz crystals. Draw one bigger Sei He Ki over the whole grid. Take your time with this, enjoy it and keep your focus on filling the grid with Sei He Ki symbols, Reiki, and love.

3. When the grid has completed its task, and you have found your somebody or rekindled a current relationship, you can dismantle it and cleanse the crystals so they are ready for their next mission and destroy the paper grid, sending its energy either to the universe by burning in a fireproof receptacle or to the earth by shredding and adding it to your compost or recycling.

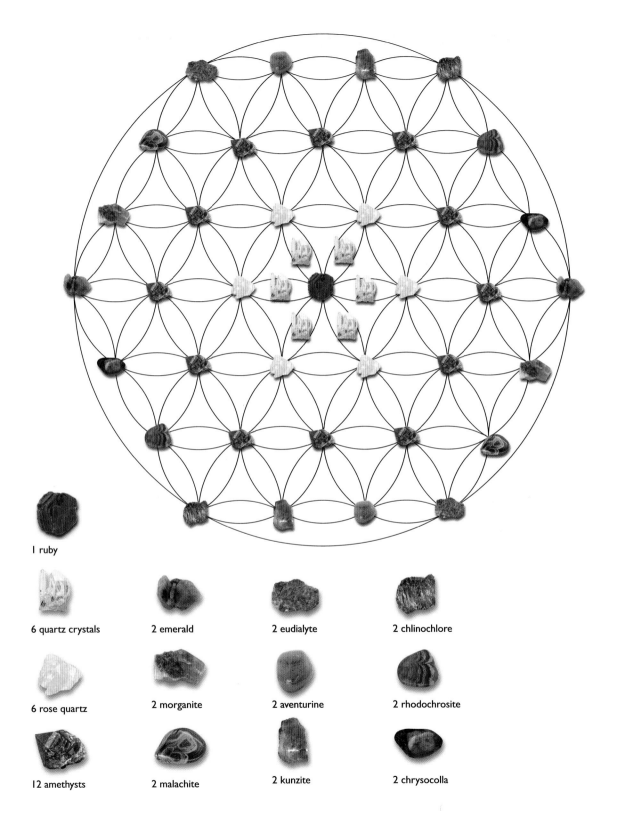

1 ruby

6 quartz crystals

2 emerald

2 eudialyte

2 chlinochlore

6 rose quartz

2 morganite

2 aventurine

2 rhodochrosite

12 amethysts

2 malachite

2 kunzite

2 chrysocolla

Crystal Reiki Healing for animals

Animals love crystals and Reiki; put them all together and your pets will adore you. Whether your companion is feeling a little out of sorts or has a serious health issue, you can help them by giving them crystals charged with Reiki in the following ways:

• Pop them in their bed so that they sleep with the healing energy.

• Put crystals in their water bowls—make sure they are thoroughly washed beforehand and avoid using crystals that are not safe to be used in water (indicated by "No elixir") by checking The Crystal Finder (see page 105).

• Put crystals in a fish tank—make sure they are thoroughly washed beforehand and always check with an expert that it is safe for fish to be exposed to them.

• Tape crystals to your pet's collar.

You can select crystals for this intuitively (see page 42) or use the Crystal Finder as a guide.

If you find your furry friend is "borrowing" your crystals, then the best thing to do is give them their own crystals. Let them play with crystals and they will indicate which ones they need. Place these crystals in their bed or sleeping area so your pet knows that they are theirs, and then you can also teach them that your crystals are yours, theirs are theirs.

A couple of other ways to help your animals are:

• Next time you are stroking or cuddling your furry friend, say "Reiki on" and let the energy flow through your hands.

• Set up the aura healing layout (see page 84), cleanse the area, and let your animals lie in it. You can also create the layout around your animal homes, such as fish tanks and bird cages, so they can benefit from the energies too.

I believe that, in the same way that we are all healers, so are our animal companions, and many of them are much more in touch with the natural world of energies than we may be. I used to have a German Shepherd Dog called Yogi who adored crystals. As he was very well trained, he spent most of his time off the leash in my shop, usually curled up behind the counter waiting for one of his human friends to come in to see him. Sometimes, for no apparent reason, he'd wander over to a specific customer he'd never seen before and sniff them in what must have been a slightly disconcerting way. Then he'd dawdle away, only to reappear a few minutes later and drop a crystal at their feet! It always turned out that they were very unwell, and this was exactly the right crystal for them. This dog grew up with crystals, sat on a floor cushion with everyone else in meditation classes, and generally lived a spiritual life. He was one of the best crystal healers I've ever known. He also chose his own crystals for self-healing, "asked" for a new one before adding it to his collection, and never buried them in the garden—that was strictly for bones!

Crystal Reiki Healing for plants

Plants are easier to care for than animals because they don't move! I usually give a crystal to a new plant when I put it in the garden to encourage it to grow well. Green moss agate and quartz are my preferred choices for this, although plants like most non-toxic crystals. Remember these crystals will be watered and release any mineral content that is water-soluble into the soil, so be sure to avoid any crystals that are not suitable for human elixirs—use The Crystal Finder (see page 105) as a guide. All you have to do is to Reiki the chosen crystal, dig the hole for the plant, pop the crystal in, and place the plant on top before filling in around it with soil. Similarly, you can put tired and broken crystals back in the ground, which is like an extended vacation for them—a chance to "get back to nature." Cleanse the crystals and give them a quick Reiki boost before putting them in the garden, spreading them among the plants.

You can also place crystals on the ground to bring positive energy. For example, I have defined my flower bed borders with large pieces of rose quartz. A large crystal can act as a focus in the garden, on a patio, or even in a planted container indoors. Your garden ornaments and sculptures could be made from crystal, or why not create a crystal rockery or waterfall, or a winding path of tumble stones? If you don't have a garden, you can still add tumble stones, crystals, and rocks to any potted plant indoors.

When placing crystals outside, be aware that some crystals such as amethyst will fade in bright direct sunlight. If in doubt, check with the store when you purchase crystals for your garden. Remember to Reiki these crystals regularly—once a month on the full moon is ideal.

To really embrace the Reiki energy in your garden, make designs of the Reiki symbols with crystals: a large Cho Ku Rei would fit in with a labyrinth on the lawn; Sei He Ki in the flowering borders brings love and therefore healthier flowers; or Hon Sha Ze Sho Nen under any fruit trees—its association with time and space connects to the seeds, which will be the future of the plant.

There are endless ways of sharing crystals with your plant friends. Your imagination is the only limit.

- You can create a quartz ladder for any climbing plants, such as passion flowers or sweet peas.

- Use a crystal rock base for a bonsai or add a crystal Buddha to it.

- Create a miniature plant and crystal scene in pots—one of my clients creates fairy houses complete with miniature live plants and crystals.

Plants love crystals and Reiki, so remember to Reiki your plant crystals each Full Moon.

CHAPTER 5

THE crystal finder

Including over 100 crystals, this chapter provides a guide to identifying your crystal by color and gives its main properties and healing benefits, including its Reiki connection and associated Reiki symbol. It will help you to identify any crystals that you may already have and to choose the crystals you want to work with. The section begins with, amethyst, ruby, and quartz because they are the three crystals that most traditionally link to Reiki and, following that, the crystals are arranged by color.

If a crystal is linked to the Dai Ko Myo symbol (see pages 32 and 36), you can use either the Usui or the Tibetan version of the symbol, depending on which one best suits your purpose; you may also choose to use the Tibetan version if you are not attuned to Reiki, as it offers more natural power.

amethyst

A variety of quartz found as crystals or masses. Its violet color is due to iron inclusions affected by natural radiation that creates color pockets. The purple/violet color can appear almost black (known as black amethyst). Other varieties include chevron amethyst with purple and white banding (see opposite), zebra amethyst, lavender amethyst, and prasiolite and amegreen (both colored green by mineral inclusions). Pink amethyst was recently discovered in Patagonia, South America, and is colored by the same process.

Common sources: Argentina (pink), Brazil, India, Madagascar, Republic of South Africa, Siberia, Uruguay

Reiki symbol: Dai Ko Myo

Chakra: crown

Reiki tip: helps you cope with responsibility, change, and public speaking, making it a favorite crystal for Reiki teachers.

HEALING QUALITIES

Physical: boosts physical energy and the immune system, helps fight bacterial or viral infection, and can be effective in the treatment of acne. Good for the heart and circulation, dissipating blood clots, as well as the lymphatic system and detoxing. Eases muscular tension. Helps when your body is physically stressed and with stress-related conditions, such as irritable bowel syndrome and migraines. Balances hormones. Cleanses the aura. Good for hearing. Recommended for insomnia as it aids a good, restful night's sleep.
Emotional/spiritual: a very relaxing and soothing crystal, it calms the nerves and relieves stress and tension. Boosts both emotional and intellectual energy, helping you cope with what the world has to throw at you. Reduces anger and violent tendencies, brings humility, balances passions, supports you through grief, and alleviates homesickness and over-sensitivity. Helps with OCD.
Other: helps negotiation skills and inspires business success.

MORE ABOUT AMETHYST

Amethyst opens and activates your crown chakra, leading to the enhancement of your own unique spiritual understanding. It helps you connect spiritually and enhances right brain activity, intuition, creativity, clairvoyance, and general sensitivity to the world around you. It also connects the crown and the heart chakras, helping you to experience spiritual love.

It can be especially helpful in the treatment of addictions, as it cleanses the blood of the addictive substance and helps to alleviate the root cause of the addiction in the emotional, mental, or spiritual body. The addiction can be physical—chemical, psychological, or behavioral. Its use in the treatment of alcoholism has been known since at least Roman times. By cleansing

the body—cleaning the body energetically—amethyst can also help in the treatment of many allergic reactions, such as asthma and hay fever, and alleviate their symptoms.

Amethyst is a fantastic pick-me-up if you're feeling generally run-down or low. It can help you make changes in your life, especially if you're feeling stuck in any way.

It's the go-to crystal for any headache. People drawn to Reiki are often empathic and sensitive to energies, which are great qualities for a healer. However, it also means Reiki people are more susceptible to disruptive energy and likely to suffer from headaches. To treat migraines and other acute headaches, hold a very dark amethyst as close as you can to the source of the pain; for milder or recurring chronic headaches, try carrying or wearing a paler amethyst. Do all the things that would normally help, such as lying down in a dark, quiet place, and you will find even the most severe headache will ease quite quickly (within 20–30 minutes). You will also find that charging an amethyst crystal with Reiki and carrying this with you 24/7 will reduce the frequency and severity of the headaches.

CHEVRON AMETHYST

Also known as banded amethyst, chevron amethyst is excellent in the relief of chronic pain. It takes the edge off the pain, allowing sufferers to do many more physical things in their life that they had been prevented from doing by the pain.

A rare inclusion in amethyst is goethite; this combination brings beauty into your auric field. You see beauty in everything around you and beauty seems to be drawn toward you.

REIKI IDEALS

Amethyst provides a perfect connection to Reiki ideals, inspiring humility and kindness on all levels. This is a simplified version of Usui Sensei's Reiki ideals (for the full version, see page 17):

Do not anger.

Do not worry.

Be humble.

Be honest.

Be compassionate.

ruby

One of the hardest substances on Earth which crystallizes in the form of tabular and rhombohedral prismatic crystals. Rubies can be any shade of red.

Common sources: India, Madagascar, Myanmar, Thailand

Reiki symbols: Sei He Ki, Hon Sha Ze Sho Nen

Chakra: heart

Reiki tip: grounds the emotion of love, bringing it into everything you do, and connects the physical to the spiritual.

HEALING QUALITIES

Physical: good for the heart, circulation, anemia, bleeding and blood loss, low blood pressure, and detoxing. Boosts the immune system and helps to fight infection. Increases physical energy. Helps all types of tissue repair, from a minor bruise to recovering from major surgery. Good for a healthy menstrual cycle. Beneficial for the health of the embryo.

Emotional/spiritual: boosts passion in all areas of your life. good for mental health and healing, the will to live, and creativity. Balances emotions and enhances sensitivity to energy. Helps with clairvoyance, past-life recall, protection, decision making, new beginnings, and change. Dispels anguish, distress, and a sense of suffering. Protects from nightmares and promotes dreams. Aids connection to spirit guides, astral travel, remote viewing, peak experiences in meditation, and rebirth. Brings health, wealth, and longevity.

MORE ABOUT RUBY

Ruby stimulates the heart chakra, opening you to receiving and sharing love. Its nurturing energy works fantastically with Reiki to bring health, spiritual knowledge, and wisdom into your world, as well as abundance and wealth. It can help you see a new pathway or direction in your life, and can transmute negative feelings into positivity. This comes about quite naturally as ruby balances the heart chakra. Reiki Masters often place ruby in their attunement room and under students' chairs to aid the connection to and open the heart chakra during the attunement.

Ruby connects to the Reiki story, bringing a realization that there is a balance between the physical and spiritual. Usui Sensei realized this himself on his path to discover Reiki and it is an integral part of Reiki teaching. Ruby is excellent when employed for distant healing (see page 93).

(see page 93)

Legend has it that ruby was employed as a casting stone to assist in decision making. It was also said that if you keep a ruby with you, your wealth would never leave you. This might be where the belief that wearing or carrying a ruby protects you from unhappiness, bad dreams, and lightning. Incidentally, I think scientifically this may be the case, as I cannot find any reports of someone wearing a ruby in fact being struck by lightning. The Bible quotes ruby as one of the stones on the breastplate of the High Priest.

A ruby will help you bring spiritual energy into all areas of your life.

RECORD KEEPER RUBIES

These are ruby crystals with one or more raised triangles on the surface, and are particularly adept at helping you access the Akashic Records.

STAR RUBIES

When polished, these display an asterism resembling a star, and are good for cleansing and focusing energy, and bringing enlightenment.

quartz crystal

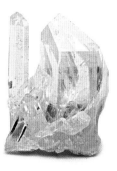

Quartz is the most common mineral found on Earth; almost 78% of the planet's surface is made up of it in one form or another. However, good-quality quartz crystals are rare. These crystallize as clear or white prismatic hexagonal crystals. It is also found in the form of druses, grains, and massive rock (known as quartzite).

Common alternative names: clear quartz, rock crystal, crystal

Common sources: Brazil, China, Madagascar, Republic of South Africa, Russia, Tibet, USA (specifically Arkansas)

Reiki symbols: all

Chakras: all

Reiki tip: supercharges Reiki by amplifying and focusing its power.

HEALING QUALITIES

Physical: good for pain relief, MS and CFS/ME. Helps with breathing, vision, hearing, tinnitus and balance, diabetes, general health of the heart, obesity, weight loss, and a healthy spine.

Emotional/spiritual: gives you a boost when you are feeling run down. Enhances both heart and brow chakras, strengthening emotions and stimulating positive thoughts. Aids meditation and counteracts negativity.

MORE ABOUT QUARTZ

Quartz lifts you up and makes you feel better. It brings light into your life, makes you happier, re-energizes you, clears your mind, brings a breath of fresh air, and improves the quality of your life. It is often called "the healing crystal" because it will channel any energy and help in almost any situation. It will alleviate the pain and distress of most physical, mental, emotional, or spiritual conditions. The problem this creates for me is not what to include here, but what to omit. Quartz can store, focus, transform, amplify, transfer, and transmit Reiki; with this thought, I will try to keep the information

relevant to this. Having said that, quartz is the most amazing panacea of the crystal world; there is often a precise variety of crystal that could be better in any specific situation, but if you have any doubt, you can always turn to quartz to help you.

Healing practices associated with quartz are recorded in some of humankind's oldest writings. It has been applied to heal sickness and wounds, it allows communication with spirits and gods, and it exhibits scientifically verifiable properties, such as the piezoelectric effect and solid-state electric fields. People throughout history have observed quartz channeling and focusing light, and that light is literally the fabric of our existence—many traditions say we are "beings of light," "we come from the light," or something similar. When a quantum physicist sees the future, she reveals a universe made not of solid matter, but simply photons of light. Through her eyes we are indeed beings of light.

Quartz is also known as the "stone of meditation," as it supports you to find and maintain a meditative state. Through meditation it can bring love, peace, serenity, mental focus, concentration, humility, clarity of thought, improved memory, and a greater awareness of energy and the world around you. It helps empty your mind, releases worries, and produces a feeling of oneness.

Some Reiki Masters work with a quartz crystal to draw the symbols in attunements, and once you are attuned to these, you can draw them over clients, Crystal Reiki Healing grids, and around your home and workplace to clear and cleanse unhelpful energies. Quartz crystal clusters can serve like an energy cleanser and create a healing environment—the perfect setting for Crystal Reiki Healing treatments.

RED

RED JASPER

A massive variety of quartz which is colored red by iron inclusions.

Common sources: Brazil, India

Reiki symbol: Raku

Chakra: base

Reiki tip: protects you from picking up empathic pains from clients.

HEALING QUALITIES

Physical: helps blood flow, breathing, and our ancient survival mechanisms. Good for athletes and all sportspeople. Prevents illness, acts as a general tonic, and keeps you healthy.

Emotional/spiritual: offers protection (when paired with jet). Encourages survival instinct. Good for rebirth, integrating new ideas, meditation, dream recall, and grounding.

GARNET

Found as dodecahedral and trapezohedral crystals, masses, and layered "plates." Colors include red, pink (eudialyte), pink/red (rhodolite), green (grossularite), emerald green (uvarovite), black (melanite), orange (spessartine), red/purple (almandine), greenish yellow (andradite), and yellow and brown (hessonite).

Common sources: India, Russia, USA

Reiki symbol: Sei He Ki

Chakras: heart and base

Reiki tip: in emotional times you can create the Sei He Ki symbol with small garnets on the heart chakra.

HEALING QUALITIES

Physical: helps with arthritis, rheumatism, detox, blood flow, raising low blood pressure, red blood cell production and associated anemia, blood disorders, underactive thyroid, vitality, and deficiencies of iodine, calcium, magnesium, and vitamins A, D, and E. Enhances health of the spine and spinal fluid, bones, heart, lungs, eyes, liver, and pancreas, Aids all conditions requiring regeneration and repair of tissues by enhancing blood flow to damaged tissue and removing toxins, as well as wounds and post-operative healing.

Emotional/spiritual: gives you the courage and strength to persevere in difficult times. Brings emotional balance, creative energy, abundance, and awareness. Helps with depression, balancing sex drive, and dealing with change, emotional trauma, chaos, disruption, the dying process and death, and end-of-life care. Connected to rejuvenation, youthfulness, magic, spiritual devotion, flow, aura, meditation, love, and a connection to your higher self. Good for people who work with numbers. Opens up the possibilities for travel.

FALCON'S EYE

A type of quartz which has replaced fibrous crocidolite, leaving a stone exhibiting chatoyancy, due to its fibrous structure and colored red, mainly by iron oxide.

Common alternative name: red tiger's eye

Common source: Republic of South Africa

Reiki symbol: Cho Ku Rei

Chakra: base

Reiki tip: works well for Usui and Tibetan Reiki Masters practicing psychic surgery.

HEALING QUALITIES

Physical: good for both male and female reproductive systems, fertility, and relief from sunburn.
Emotional/spiritual: helps to ignite an emotional spark and connect to sexuality. Encourages you to be practical and do things, rather than just thinking about them. Good for understanding the reasons underlying any problem.

MOOKAITE

A patterned red and cream variety of jasper. Smaller pieces may only show one color.

Common source: Australia

Reiki symbol: Raku

Chakra: base

Reiki tip: keep mookaite with you if you are treating children, as it helps you tune into their energy and understand them.

HEALING QUALITIES

Physical: good for the thyroid, weight loss, and stomach health. Helps with hernias and water retention.
Emotional/spiritual: good for grounding, self-esteem, dreams, meditation, perception, communication, calming, protection, decisions, and new ideas. Helps you cope with fear, depression, loneliness, and caring for children. Aids job seeking and creativity. Helps you find direction in your life and move forward along your chosen path.

RED CALCITE

A variety of massive calcite.

Common source: Mexico

Reiki symbol: Sei He Ki

Chakra: base

Reiki tip: place this under your therapy bed for nervous clients.

HEALING QUALITIES

Physical: calms physical energy and helps with ADHD, water absorption, and stress-related diarrhea.
Emotional/spiritual: good for grounding, panic attacks, anxiety, OCD, stress, and nervousness. Quickly calms most situations.

ORANGE

CARNELIAN

A variety of chalcedony that forms orange pebbles.

Common alternative names: cornelian, sard

Common sources: worldwide (especially Brazil, India, and Uruguay)

Reiki symbol: Cho Ku Rei

Chakra: sacral

Reiki tip: when you're feeling drained, sit down and hold a carnelian for 10 minutes.

HEALING QUALITIES

Physical: helps with breathing disorders, asthma, hay fever, blood oxygenation, balance, common colds, digestion, vitality, infections, jaundice, memory, neuralgia, bronchitis, speech, tissue regeneration, CFS/ME, and minor cuts and grazes (as a topical elixir). Enhances the health of the gall bladder, liver, lungs, kidneys, pancreas, voice, spine, spleen, and thyroid.

Emotional/spiritual: brings an energy boost and is a feel-better stone. Balances appetite as needed, good for eating disorders, and reduces thirst. Helps with managing anger, envy, fear, rage, sorrow, confusion, jealousy, apathy, lethargy, and laziness. Brings focus, courage, compassion, personal power, self-esteem, and confidence. Linked to study, inspiration, connection to spirit, meditation retreats, and inquisitiveness. Helps you to see the links between dis-ease and emotions so you can deal with the emotions and prevent disease. The combination of confidence, courage, and energy boost makes this a particularly good stone for live performers such as actors and musicians.

ORANGE CALCITE

Bright to pale orange rocks.

Common source: Mexico

Reiki symbol: Dai Ko Myo

Chakra: sacral

Reiki tip: place orange calcite in business meeting rooms to ease the atmosphere.

HEALING QUALITIES

Physical: balances energy so both physically calming and energizing as required, and good for vitality.
Emotional/spiritual: brings inspiration, laughter, and joy. Calms aggression, belligerence, pugnaciousness, and hostility.

CROCOITE

Prismatic orange crystals, masses, and aggregates.

Common source: Australia

Reiki symbol: Dai Ko Myo

Chakra: sacral

Reiki tip: a great support for all types of change—emotional, mental, physical, and spiritual.

HEALING QUALITIES

Physical: good for the reproductive system and managing death, dying, and end-of-life care.
Emotional/spiritual: promotes intuition and creativity. Boosts sexuality. Excellent to help with big and difficult decisions and life changes, which is why it's nicknamed "The divorce stone." Relieves distress and calms emotions. NO ELIXIR.

VANADINITE

Barrel-shaped and hollow prismatic crystals and masses.

Common source: Morocco

Reiki symbol: Sei He Ki

Chakra: sacral

Reiki tip: helps you cognitively understand why things happen.

HEALING QUALITIES

Physical: helps with breathing and breath control so good for asthma and lung health. Also good for bladder health.
Emotional/spiritual: good for meditation, goal setting, and coping with exhaustion. Helps spendaholics rein in their habit. Aids your thought process.
NO ELIXIR.

HALITE

Salt crystals, massive or cubic, clear, single, or multicolored, which occur in orange, yellow/red/blue, pink, and green.

Common sources: Australia (green), Germany (blue), Pakistan (specifically Himalayas—orange), USA (pinks and red)

Reiki symbol: Raku

Chakra: sacral

Reiki tip: can be employed to mark a special space for healing or attunements.

HEALING QUALITIES

Physical: balances bodily fluids. Good for colon, intestinal, and kidney health, water retention, and endurance.
Emotional/spiritual: helps with mood swings and bipolar disorder.
NO ELIXIR.

TANGERINE QUARTZ

A quartz crystal which is colored orange to orange-red by hematite that is naturally bonded to the surface.

Common sources: Brazil, Madagascar

Reiki symbol: Cho Ku Rei

Chakras: all the lower chakras—base, sacral, and solar plexus

Reiki tip: a powerful crystal to add a magical boost of energy to any healing or project.

HEALING QUALITIES

Physical: helps with weight loss, intestinal health, and absorption of vitamins and iron. Good for blood, red blood cell production, energy, reproductive system, fertility, sexual dysfunction and associated lower abdominal pain. Balances acidity, so will help with all cancerous growths/tumors, and liberates free radicals.
Emotional: helps relationships by boosting passion and emotional connection, eliminating inhibitions, and releasing the desire for physical contact. Promotes change, self-awareness, self-understanding, self-healing, growth, inner strength, forgiveness, and the courage to move forward. Helps you surpass inner turmoil and trauma and release self-defeating, self-sabotaging, self-limiting, and self-judgmental beliefs. Gives a sense of worth or self-value, allowing you to just let things go. Boosts intentions, especially those directed at love, relationships, and creativity. Supports your inner child and promotes playfulness and creativity, manifestation, and grounding ideas into practical reality. Helps emotional stress and releases tension. Offers psychic protection, bringing a sense of spiritual security, calmness, and comfort.

YELLOW

CITRINE

A yellow, golden, or lemon variety of quartz. Its color is due to heat from volcanic and other earth activity.

Common sources: Brazil, Democratic Republic of Congo

Reiki symbol: Cho Ku Rei

Chakra: solar plexus

Reiki tip: citrine helps keep the inspiration flowing and is excellent for Reiki Masters writing their teaching manuals and therapists composing advertising literature. My trusty writing crystal is a citrine.

HEALING QUALITIES

Physical: good for all of the digestive system, from your mouth to anus, and helps all related disorders, such as Crohn's disease, IBS, and colitis. Helps with energy levels, jaundice, nausea and sickness/vomiting, tissue regeneration, detox, anemia, and eyesight/vision, and the health of the heart, kidneys, liver, thyroid, and thymus.

Emotional/spiritual: brings abundance in all forms: health, wealth, and happiness. Excellent for creativity. A feel-better stone. Helps with decisions, relationships, managing anger, self-esteem, getting rid of emotional toxins, a yin/yang balance, teaching and studying (learning), problem solving, awareness, new beginnings, and repairing and strengthening the aura.

Other: helps with selling houses— known as the "money stone."

GOLDEN LABRADORITE

A golden form of feldspar displaying labradorescence.

Common alternative names: sunstone, American sunstone

Common source: USA

Reiki symbols: Dai Ko Myo, Cho Ku Rei

Chakras: solar plexus, crown

Reiki tip: brings light into the darkness, illuminating body and soul—works well for anyone experiencing dark times in their life.

HEALING QUALITIES

Physical: good for right/left brain balance (magic and science, intuition and intellect), which brings understanding.

Emotional: promotes self-confidence. Uplifting, bringing lightness and a positive sense of purpose to you and everything and everyone around you, as if adding captured golden hues of sunshine to your life. Good for creativity, inspiration, originality, and new beginnings.

COPPER

A metal that forms freeform shapes, dendrites, plates, and rhombohedral crystals.

Common source: USA

Reiki symbol: Cho Ku Rei

Chakra: sacral

Reiki tip: channels energy exceptionally well—Reiki a piece of copper (see page 38) and give it to a friend or client in need of a boost.

HEALING QUALITIES

Physical: helps with circulation, physical exhaustion, lethargy, general malaise, tiredness, detox, and vitality. Protects against and eases symptoms of poisoning. Good for infected wounds and stimulating metabolism. joint conditions, such as inflammation and bursitis, and, with chrysocolla, can treat arthritis and rheumatism.

Emotional/spiritual: a feel-better stone that brings emotional balance. Eases emotional exhaustion by boosting chi, and calms restlessness and over-excitability. Connected to sexuality and enhances libido.

BALTIC AMBER

Fossilized resin from prehistoric trees that may have inclusions of animal and/or plant material. Colors include yellow to orange and brown (most common—around 70% of natural amber), red, green, blue, black (may be very dark red or brown), and white.

Only source: Baltic Sea area	
Reiki symbol: Hon Sha Ze Sho Nen	
Chakra: solar plexus	
Reiki tip: helps to heal the past—issues from childhood and past lives.	

HEALING QUALITIES

Physical: helps with acne, constipation (as an elixir), detox, heart health, hormones, post-op healing, asthma, and throat, kidney and bladder conditions. As a topical elixir, it acts as a disinfectant and antiseptic for bacterial infections.

Emotional/spiritual: provides an ancient connection to release past trauma, fear, and hurt, so good for past-life healing and recall. Calming and helps with childhood issues, memory, absent-mindedness, recovery from abuse, releasing trapped emotions and negativity, yin/yang balance, bipolar disorder, and schizophrenia. Encourages fulfilment of dreams and goals. Symbolizes renewal of marriage vows (like an eternity ring). Cleanses spaces and removes negativity, so perfect for healing, workshop, and therapy rooms. When worn, helps to purify body, mind, and spirit.

YELLOW JASPER

A yellow variety of chalcedony.

Common source: Republic of South Africa	
Reiki symbol: Sei He Ki	
Chakra: solar plexus	
Reiki tip: can help you understand the underlying cause of disease.	

HEALING QUALITIES

Physical: good for digestion, especially absorbing nutrients, and boosts energy.

Emotional/spiritual: gives protection for travelers. Encourages intellectual pursuits and digestion of ideas, leading to greater understanding.

TIGER'S EYE

Quartz replacing asbestos (blue is called crocidolite; "ordinary" is golden) that shows chatoyancy due to the fibrous structure. Colors include gold/yellow/brown, blue (hawk's eye), and red (falcon's eye).

Only source: Republic of South Africa	
Reiki symbol: Cho Ku Rei	
Chakra: solar plexus	
Reiki tip: helpful to release a nervous client's inhibitions.	

HEALING QUALITIES

Physical: good for the whole digestive system and digestive disorders and illnesses, including flatulence, nausea, and diverticulosis. Helps eye health, eye diseases, nocturnal vision, and broken bones.

Emotional/spiritual: gives courage to work through challenging times and achieve life's goals—a "go for it" stone! Releases inhibitions and helps with introversion, fear, negativity, narrow-mindedness, grounding, and absent/distant healing. Sharpens the mind and taps into intuition and gut feeling, so is good for investigations (helping people such as police, scientists, insurers, and accountants), depression, balance, new beginnings, wealth, A feel-better stone that brings balance (including of yin/yang and right/left brain) and calm. Eases turmoil and dispels worry. Good for people who are deliberately obstructive.

GOLDEN HEALER QUARTZ

Yellowish iron coating on or included within quartz crystals.

Common alternative names: golden quartz, yellow quartz (this is a misnomer)

Common source: worldwide (see quartz, page 109)

Reiki symbol: Sei He Ki

Chakras: all, especially heart

Reiki tip: try working with this crystal for your own self-healing.

HEALING QUALITIES

Physical: helps energy flow through meridians thereby supporting all physical healing and the immune system. Helps to repair skin damage including burns, sunburn, cuts, and grazes.

Emotional/spiritual: eases energy shifts and facilitates all emotional healing. Good for strengthening the aura, removing unhealthy blocks to lifestyle changes, and behavior patterns. Releases fear, past hurts, and self-judgmental thoughts, and is particularly helpful if you feel that you're not worth the good things in life. Attracts abundance and prosperity, and is good for relationships, cutting ties with

the past, cutting cords, bringing emotional balance, and restoring your self-esteem after disappointment. Cleanses, clears, reboots; a stone of rebirth. It's a happy crystal that will help you to walk your walk through life. Heals rooms holding traumatic energy. Balances yin/yang.

LIBYAN GOLD TEKTITE

A variety of tektite, which is meteoritic glass created from the immense heat of a meteorite impact with the Earth. The heat is so intense that both the meteorite and the Earth's surface are melted, and tektite is formed as this mixture of space material and Earth cool together. Libyan gold tektite is the only rare yellow variety; more common are black or brown tektites, and a rare green variety, moldavite.

Common alternative names:
Libyan desert glass, Libyan glass

Only source: Sahara Desert (Libya)

Reiki symbol: Hon Sha Ze Sho Nen

Chakra: crown

Reiki tip: connects through time and space, just like the symbol it is linked to, Hon Sha Ze Sho Nen.

HEALING QUALITIES

Physical: good for circulation, fever, dehydration, prolonged exposure to inclement weather, and fertility (specifically ovulation).

Emotional: good for yin/yang balance, creativity leading to artistic abundance, reasoning, telepathy and ESP, psychic surgery, meditation (reaching and maintaining peak experience), distant healing, and contact with other worlds. Reorganizes chaotic circumstances and is particularly good when you feel your world is collapsing around you. Aids connection with distant friends and family.

GREEN

MALACHITE

Crystalline aggregates, druses, botryoidal structures, and clusters of radiating fibrous crystals. Single prismatic crystals are rare. More common are malachite pseudomorphs of azurite, which produce a more tabular crystal. Color is green, often with various shades of green and black bands.

Common sources: Democratic Republic of Congo, USA

Reiki symbol: Sei He Ki

Chakra: heart

Reiki tip: excellent for emotional healing—it is like taking a sledgehammer to the walls we build.

HEALING QUALITIES

Physical: a good all-round healer. Helps with asthma, arthritis, broken bones, epilepsy, eyesight, endurance, inflammation, rheumatism, swelling, tissue regeneration, tumors, torn muscles, immune system, and detox, plus health of blood, heart, pancreas, pituitary gland, spleen, and teeth. Eases birth and has antiseptic properties.
Emotional/spiritual: quick, strong, and bold emotional clearing. Calming and brings emotional balance and restful sleep. Helps with insomnia, dream interpretation, depression, bipolar disorder, and meditation.
NO ELIXIR

AVENTURINE

A variety of quartz with inclusions of mica, giving a speckled or sparkly effect. Commonly green; other colors include blue, white, red/peach, and brown.

Common sources: Brazil, India

Reiki symbol: Sei He Ki

Chakra: heart

Reiki tip: great for stopping your energy being sucked out of you by "energy vampires."

HEALING QUALITIES

Physical: a go-to crystal for all muscle injuries and problems. Good for health of lungs, heart, adrenal glands, and urogenital system, and helps reaction speed, so good for sportspeople.
Emotional/spiritual: calming and relaxing. Protects and soothes emotions. Helps with pre-exam and exam stress, creativity, motivation, yin/yang balance, decisions, leadership, and connecting to spirit guides. Brings success.

GREEN MOSS AGATE

Transparent or translucent green, white, and clear moss-like patterned masses of agate. Also occurs in red, yellow, brown, black, and blue.

Common source: India

Reiki symbol: Sei He Ki

Chakra: heart

Reiki tip: helps to release buried emotions.

HEALING QUALITIES

Physical: good for detoxing, the immune system, dehydration, eyes, fungal infections, digestion, cold and flu symptoms, and skin disorders (as topical elixir).
Emotional/spiritual: helps with anxiety, stress, and tension. Brings wealth.
Other: great for the healthy development and growth of plants, new crops, houseplants, gardens, and trees.

JADE

Forms as masses in many colors, including green, orange, brown, blue, cream, white, lavender, red, gray, and black. Types of jade include jadeite and nephrite.

Common sources: Canada, China, Myanmar, USA

Reiki symbol: Dai Ko Myo

Chakra: heart

Reiki tip: a very feminine crystal for all reproductive and menstrual issues.

HEALING QUALITIES

Physical: helps with acne, asthma, lymphatic system, bacterial and viral infections, eye disorders, immune system, longevity, general malaise, and health of joints (particularly hips), bones, gallbladder, heart, kidneys, muscles, spleen, and bladder. Lowers high blood pressure. Good for female reproductive system including fallopian tubes, fertility, ovaries, menstrual cycle, menstruation, period pains, PMS, vagina, and womb. Also good for skin and hair (as an elixir).
Emotional/spiritual: brings wisdom to decisions you need to make. Helps those who are accident prone. Encourages balance (particularly emotional), confidence, courage, and compassion. Helps with grounding, justice, modesty, negativity, schizophrenia, and solving problems. Promotes dreams and dream recall (place under pillow). Encourages dreams, goals, and ideals. Offers connection to ancient civilizations and wisdom, protection, peace (both inner and outer), and shamanic access to spirit worlds.
Other: traditional child's first stone to bring wisdom, luck, and longevity.

CLINOCHLORE

Chlorite mineral that forms green/white, colorless, and yellow masses and, occasionally, crystals.

Common alternative name: seraphinite

Common source: Russia

Reiki symbol: Sei He Ki

Chakra: heart

Reiki tip: helps you to connect to your Reiki guide(s).

HEALING QUALITIES

Physical: stabilizes critical conditions.
Emotional/spiritual: good for relationships, a broken heart, fear of the unknown, connection with angels and guardians, nurturing, and spiritual love.

CHRYSOCOLLA

Occurs as layers, masses, botryoidal structures, and druses.

Common sources: Peru, USA

Reiki symbol: Dai Ko Myo

Chakra: heart

Reiki tip: the go-to crystal for arthritis, especially when combined with copper.

HEALING QUALITIES

Physical: good for digestion, hips, joints, arthritis, rheumatism, metabolism, period pains, PMS, female sexuality, thyroid, high blood pressure, pancreas, diabetes (insulin production and blood sugar levels), muscles and muscle cramps (especially in the arms and legs), restless leg syndrome, blood disorders (such as leukemia), lungs, lung conditions (such as TB, asthma, bronchitis, and emphysema), oxidation of the blood, ease of breathing, and increased lung capacity. Prevents ulcers. Promotes healthy development of the fetus and babies.

Emotional/spiritual: a feel-better stone that helps with earth healing, stressful situations, releasing negative emotions, and revitalizing relationships, as well as creativity, guilt, phobias, and tension. Helps to heal a broken heart. A good crystal for those who have a habit of "putting their foot in it."

GREEN CALCITE
Bright emerald green to pale green masses.

Common source: Mexico

Reiki symbol: Sei He Ki

Chakra: heart

Reiki tip: if you have a nervous client, place a chunky green calcite crystal in each of their hands at the start of the treatment.

HEALING QUALITIES

Physical: aids the prevention and treatment of infection. Calms nervous twitches.
Emotional/spiritual: very calming and acts quickly, so excellent for panic attacks and easing anxiety. Helps you cope when others are laughing at you.

UVAROVITE
Emerald green variety of garnet.

Common source: Russia

Reiki symbol: Sei He Ki

Chakra: heart

Reiki tip: if you are a Reiki Master, place this in your teaching space, as it helps inspire teachers to speak from the heart.

HEALING QUALITIES

Physical: good for detox and heart and lung health. Helps with acidosis, leukemia, and kidney and bladder infections.
Emotional/spiritual: calming and good for the soul. Alleviates loneliness. Brings together twin souls/soul mates. Helps to explore the physical aspects of love-making. Promotes clear thought, so good for teachers.

UNAKITE
A mixture of epidote, feldspar, and quartz.

Common source: South Africa

Reiki symbol: Sei He Ki

Chakras: base, heart

Reiki tip: connects base and heart chakras, allowing you to "move forward from your heart"—act from your heart, your own truth or perception of what you believe.

HEALING QUALITIES

Physical: encourages weight gain. Good for heart health, fertility, pregnancy, and the healthy development of the fetus.
Emotional/spiritual: helps with emotions, yin/yang balance, and grief— whether associated with the loss of a loved one or especially for the loss of an idea, dream, goal, or concept. Good for being in the present moment, accepting past experiences, accessing past lives, avoiding blocks you put in your own way, and identifying the cause of dis-ease.

EMERALD

Green gem variety of beryl.

Common sources: Columbia for gem quality, Brazil for commercial grade

Reiki symbol: Sei He Ki

Chakra: heart

Reiki tip: make emerald the focus stone in your Crystal Reiki grid to bring love into your life.

HEALING QUALITIES

Physical: helps with asthma, bacterial and viral infections, eyesight, fertility, growth, immune system, inflammation, jaundice, sores, vitality, angina, biliousness, insect bites, and high blood pressure. Good for the health of bones, heart, kidneys, liver, teeth, and bile ducts. Has antiseptic qualities.
Emotional/spiritual: promotes love on every level. Brings emotional balance. Good for spiritual growth, honesty, memory, patience, irritability, and a bad temper.

CHRYSOPRASE

Green or lemon-yellow variety of chalcedony.

Common source: Australia

Reiki symbol: Sei He Ki

Chakra: heart

Reiki tip: a great crystal to help you understand your stress or that of your client.

HEALING QUALITIES

Physical: good for spleen health, scurvy, dexterity, and fertility.
Emotional/spiritual: allows you to see through the "fog" in your mind, so good for confusion, anxiety, depression, fear, bipolar disorder, schizophrenia, neurotic patterns, and stress. Helps you to find and accept the root cause of your stress. Also helps with an inferiority or superiority complex, arrogance, judgmental attitudes, a broken heart, and sexual polarities. A feel-better stone that is good for balance, general mental health and healing, meditation, acceptance of others, and self-acceptance.

PERIDOT

Small green prismatic crystals and masses.

Common alternative names: chrysolite, olivine

Common sources: Afghanistan, Brazil, Canary Islands, Pakistan, Russia, Sri Lanka, USA

Reiki symbol: Sei He Ki

Chakra: heart

Reiki tip: peridot helps to get things moving again, whether in a digestive sense or a life path.

HEALING QUALITIES

Physical: aids cancer treatment; peridot balances acidity and therefore it can be helpful in the treatment of any tumor because the healthy cells around the growth become acidic. Good for the health of the heart, lungs, spleen, liver, pancreas, colon, gallbladder, and intestines. Good for digestion and helps with acid reflux, detoxing, constipation, gastroenteritis, IBS, and Crohn's disease. Helps with sunburn, ulcers, promoting weight gain, astigmatism,

and near-sightedness. Acts as a general physical tonic. Stimulates contractions during labor.

Emotional/spiritual: helpful for addictions, alcoholism, depression, emotional blockages, lethargy, laziness, mental health and healing, stress, recognizing behavior patterns and cycles, ego, anger, and jealousy. A feel-better stone. Brings protection from outside influences and enlightenment through meditation.

VERDELITE

Vertically striated prismatic green tourmaline crystals.

Common sources: Brazil, Pakistan

Reiki symbol: Sei He Ki

Chakras: heart, brow

Reiki tip: protects against picking up energies from others. This is essential when giving treatments (see Chapter 3).

HEALING QUALITIES

Physical: good for the health of the brain, eyes, heart, thymus, and immune system. Helps with constipation and encourages weight loss.

Emotional/spiritual: stops worry—worry is a phenomenal waste of energy, so many people discover this crystal is a real life-changer! Good for getting in touch with thoughts, ideas and feelings, visualization, and compassion. Helps you connect to and communicate with plants. Helps with negativity and abuse. Brings peace of mind, abundance, creativity, and success.

MOLDAVITE

Green tektite made from reformed natural glass material, originally created when a meteorite exploded just above the earth, melting itself and the earth's surface, making them part earth, part alien rock.

Common alternative name: valtavaa

Only source: Czech Republic

Reiki symbol: Hon Sha Ze Sho Nen

Chakras: brow, heart

Reiki tip: transcends time and space so helps with issues such as healing childhood or past-life issues, or healing events/trauma that may have happened in another place.

HEALING QUALITIES

Physical: a soft general tonic for the body. Brings physical and mental balance.

Emotional/spiritual: opens the mind to new possibilities. Good for new experiences. Assisted altered mind states such as meditation, dreams, and hypnosis. Good for clairsentience.

PINK

ROSE QUARTZ

Pink crystalline masses and, rarely, small hexagonal crystals.

Common sources: Brazil, India, Madagascar, Republic of South Africa

Reiki symbol: Sei He Ki

Chakra: heart

Reiki tip: don't be fooled by this crystal's soft and gentle reputation—it can dig deep into any emotional turmoil.

HEALING QUALITIES

Physical: good for fertility and menstrual cycles, and the skin, including complexion, a youthful appearance, and wrinkles. Helps with asthma, circulation, general aches and pains, varicose veins, detoxing, vertigo, coughs, flu, burns, and sunburn, and the health of the heart, blood, kidneys, spleen, and adrenal glands.

Emotional/spiritual: calming, like a spa day for the emotions. Promotes love on all levels. Good for relationships, romance, tapping into female energy and qualities, balancing sex drive and sexual frustration. Helpful for a crisis, anger, stress, tension, fear, forgiveness, guilt, grief, feelings of inadequacy, jealousy, and resentment, upset, emotional wounds (the feeling of being wounded), and phobias. Helps you connect to childhood experiences, emotions, creativity, art, music, writing, and your imagination.

MORGANITE

A pink variety of beryl that forms hexagonal prismatic crystals, usually with flat terminations.

Common sources: Brazil, Pakistan

Reiki symbol: Sei He Ki

Chakra: heart

Reiki tip: Reiki Masters can bring this into the attunement space to boost the heart connection with their students.

HEALING QUALITIES

Physical: helps oxygenate blood so can aid all physical healing, but especially conditions affecting the chest and lungs, such as asthma and emphysema.

Emotional/spiritual: fills the space left in the heart by a loss, such as a broken relationship or bereavement. Promotes love and opens a narrow mind, so reduces racism, sexism, and other -isms. Good for contact with spirit guides, a calm mind, meditation, wisdom, ceremonies, and time management. Allows you to see things from a different perspective with clearer thought.

EUDIALYTE

A variety of pink garnet that is often intermingled with other minerals.

Common source: Russia

Reiki symbol: Sei He Ki

Chakra: heart

Reiki tip: works well in combination with morganite.

HEALING QUALITIES

Physical: good for eye disorders (especially stress-related), the heart, and circulation.

Emotional/spiritual: opens the heart—firstly to release trapped emotions from the past, then to allow love to flow unhindered. Lets you connect with the past, childhood, and past lives. Good for self-love, forgiveness, and ESP. Can ease the discomfort that often comes with change.

KUNZITE

A pink variety of spodumene that forms flattened, vertically striated prismatic crystals. Crystals can be bi- or tri-colored.

Common source: Afghanistan

Reiki symbol: Sei He Ki

Chakra: heart

Reiki tip: helps all stress-related conditions.

HEALING QUALITIES

Physical: good for the heart, blood pressure, lungs, period pains, hormone secretion, skin, and a youthful appearance.

Emotional/spiritual: the go-to crystal for easing addictions, whether physical or behavioral, such as compulsive behavior, OCD, and stopping smoking. Calming, centering, and helps with balancing desire, control of emotions, depression, PMS, female sexuality, self-esteem, expressing love, meditation, and immaturity. Removes obstacles from your path, allowing your energy to flow to people and projects, as well as negativity in the environment and energy blocks causing physical dis-ease. Offers energy protection and is a feel-better stone.

RUBELLITE

Vertically striated prismatic pink to red tourmaline crystals.

Common alternative name: pink tourmaline

Common source: Brazil

Reiki symbol: Sei He Ki

Chakras: base, heart

Reiki tip: brings compassion when explaining your understanding of a client's condition.

HEALING QUALITIES

Physical: good for vitality, fertility, the digestive and reproductive systems, heart, lungs, pancreas, and blood vessels.

Emotional/spiritual: encourages creativity and survival skills. Good for tactfulness and helps bring a diplomatic approach to any situation (so good for politicians). Brings protection.

COBALTOAN CALCITE

Occurs as drusy crusts and spherical masses. Sometimes found with or near malachite.

Common alternative name: cobaltocalcite

Common sources: Democratic Republic of Congo, Morocco

Reiki symbol: Sei He Ki

Chakras: heart, throat, brow, crown

Reiki tip: hold this if you're feeling overwhelmed, overworked, or undervalued.

HEALING QUALITIES

Physical: good for eyesight and the heart.
Emotional/spiritual: lets you to see the beauty in everyone, everything, and every situation you encounter and to recognize and learn each lesson along your path. Brings happiness, and helps you find your inner truth and discover your life purpose. Helps with emotional expression and helps your desires become reality. Draws out inner hurts and emotional pain. Helps relieve depression and despair.

RHODOCHROSITE

Found as masses, druses, botryoidal structures, and, rarely, small rhombohedral crystals. Commonly, the color ranges from pale pink to deep red. When tumble-polished, it usually has attractive pink and white bands.

Common sources: Argentina, Peru

Reiki symbol: Sei He Ki

Chakra: heart

Reiki tip: rhodochrosite can bring passion to every aspect of your life.

HEALING QUALITIES

Physical: good for the circulation, heart, kidneys, CFS/ME, and spleen. Promotes the healthy development of babies.
Emotional/spiritual: helps with nervous or mental breakdown, courage, inner strength, memory, passion, 21st-century stress, emotional trauma, aging, music, sex, and yin/yang balance. Helps things flow.

RAINBOW

RAINBOW FLUORITE

Cubic, octahedral, and rhombododecahedral crystals and masses. Colors may include green, purple, blue, and clear/colorless bands in the same specimen.

Common source: China

Reiki symbol: Cho Ku Rei

Chakra: brow

Reiki tip: focuses the mind in any situation.

HEALING QUALITIES

Physical: good for bones, backache and lumbago, and the immune system. Protects against disease and helps to keep you well—in particular, protects carers working with those who have infectious diseases.
Emotional/spiritual: helps with eating disorders (such as anorexia and bulimia), overexcitement, stress, decisions, concentration, and relationships. Brings order out of chaos. Good for groups and meditation.

TITANIUM QUARTZ

A quartz crystal that is bonded with titanium and niobium.

Common alternative names: flame aura quartz, rainbow quartz, rainbow aura quartz, aura quartz, royal aura

Common source: USA (from Arkansas or Brazilian quartz), at the time of writing there is relatively new production in China, so far, the quality is significantly lower

Reiki symbol: Dai Ko Myo

Chakras: all, but especially crown

Reiki tip: gives color to the flow of energy. It is unhealthy for energy to be static (whether that's always feeling energized or having very little energy)—it is supposed to go up and down.

HEALING QUALITIES

Physical: good for managing a fever, body fluids (such as dehydration and water retention), bone cancer, and MS. Prevents illness (i.e. keeps you well when you are healthy).
Emotional/spiritual: helps you see another's point of view and find your own true path through life. Assists meditation, change, and career decisions. Stimulates energy flow. Helps you see auras. Centers emotions when you feel "all over the place." A feel-better stone.

ANGEL AURA QUARTZ

A quartz crystal that is bonded with platinum and silver.

Common alternative name: opal aura

Common source: USA (from Arkansas or Brazilian quartz), at the time of writing there is relatively new production in China, so far, the quality is significantly lower

Reiki symbol: Dai Ko Myo

Chakras: all

Reiki tip: helps you call on your Reiki guides, angels, and guardians to help with healing.

HEALING QUALITIES

Physical: prevents minor illnesses (i.e. keeping you well when you are healthy).

Emotional/spiritual: linked to aura, karma (good for karmic healing), love, peace, and harmony. Helps with protection, accessing akashic records, connecting to the angelic realms, nurturing, and empathy. Good for those in caring professions.

WATERMELON TOURMALINE

Vertically striated prismatic green or blue tourmaline with a pink or red center running through part or all of the crystal. Often presented as slices, which make it look like watermelon.

Common sources: Brazil, Pakistan

Reiki symbol: Sei He Ki

Chakra: heart

Reiki tip: helps you to see the funny side of any situation.

HEALING QUALITIES

Physical: good for the heart, lungs, reflexes, and absorption of food.

Emotional/spiritual: helps you connect to your higher self. Encourages fun and humor, love, and emotions. Good for discretion, nervousness, those

who are accident prone, communication, and travel. Brings stillness and synchronicity. Helps you feel better from the bottom of your heart.

LABRADORITE

Plagioclase feldspar with albite that occurs as masses. Gray-green in color with brilliant flashes of blue, red, gold, purple, and green, due to light interference within the structure of the minerals' composition.

Common alternative names: black moonstone, labrador moonstone, labrador feldspar, spectrolite

Common sources: Canada, Madagascar, Norway

Reiki symbol: Raku

Chakra: crown

Reiki tip: good to work with if you have a client whose energy feels stuck, because it enhances the flow of energy between the aura and the chakras.

HEALING QUALITIES

Physical: good for digestion and eyes. Helps with warts (hold the stone to the wart, or rub or tap the stone gently on it).

Emotional/spiritual: stabilizes the aura. Balance right/left brain activity (magic and science, intuition and intellect). Brings mental sharpness, inspiration, and originality. Allows you to see many possibilities at once. Helps with insecurity, anxiety, and stress. Allows magic to happen around you—opportunities come to you.

OPAL

Occurs as masses in a multitude of colors including white (common opal), pink, black, beige, blue, yellow, brown, orange, red, green, and purple. Shows iridescence (sometimes called fire) in various colors, which

is caused by the diffraction of light within the crystalline structure. Common opal does not have a diffraction grating in its structure and so does not show this effect.

Common sources: Australia, Ethiopia, Mexico, Peru, Tanzania, USA

Reiki symbol: Dai Ko Myo

Chakras: heart, throat, crown

Reiki tip: helps you develop your psychic abilities.

HEALING QUALITIES

Physical: helps with detoxing, infections, fever, circulation, Parkinson's disease, childbirth, and diabetes. Good for the kidneys, eyes, and vision.

Emotional/spiritual: promotes good characteristics and allows bad characteristics to come out so you can deal with them. Encourages creativity, inspiration, imagination, and shamanic visions. Reduces inhibition. Enhances memory.

AGATE

A variety of chalcedony that occurs as masses and is usually banded or patterned in many colors (see also green moss agate, blue lace agate, gray banded agate, and crazy lace agate)

Common sources: worldwide

Reiki symbol: Cho Ku Rei

Chakras: see specific agate varieties

Reiki tip: strengthens your aura and acts as a shield against unhelpful energies.

HEALING QUALITIES

Physical: good for the colon, pancreas, gastroenteritis, IBS, Crohn's disease, wind pains, circulation, lymphatic system, sight, and varicose veins.

Emotional/spiritual: encourages emotional security and energy, natural talents, and faithfulness in relationships. Balances sexual energy. Helps with channeling. Good for meditation to help diagnosis through insight.

ONYX

A multicolored, layered variety of chalcedony, found in colors including black, gray, white, blue, brown, yellow, red, and orange.

Common sources: India, Pakistan

Reiki symbol: Raku

Chakra: base

Reiki tip: good for business decisions regarding your healing practice.

HEALING QUALITIES

Physical: good for the feet.

Emotional/spiritual: enhances contact with your god. Helps with grief, lack of self-control, decisions, and yin/yang balance. Helps you take charge of situations. Brings good luck and happiness into the home. Connects you to your roots.

MULTICOLORED

CHALCEDONY

A form of quartz that occurs as masses with mineral inclusions that produce various colors, including white, pink, blue, and red, but theoretically it can be any color. Several specific varieties of chalcedony are discussed in this book—see agate, carnelian, chrysoprase, jasper, onyx, and petrified wood.

Common sources: worldwide

Reiki symbol: Sei He Ki

Chakras: see specific chalcedony varieties

Reiki tip: a very nurturing crystal for both you and your clients.

HEALING QUALITIES

Physical: helps production of bone marrow so good for blood, oxygenation etc. Helps to promote weight loss..
Emotional/spiritual: helps with childhood issues, expression, abuse, drug addiction and addictive behavior, obsessions, OCD, obesity, stress, balancing masculine and feminine traits, irritability, senility, and dementia. Helps lessen compulsions. Good for ceremonies, telepathy, and mental stability.

JASPER

A variety of opaque chalcedony that is found in red, yellow, green, brown, blue, and purple, as well as with mixed colors and patterns, such as mookaite and picture jasper.

Common sources: worldwide

Reiki symbol: Raku

Chakras: base, plus others with specific jaspers

Reiki tip: if you're feeling low before giving a treatment, meditate with jasper, as it's a good "pick-me-up."

HEALING QUALITIES

Physical: helps prevent illness, and is a general physical tonic for when you are feeling run down. Good for the bladder, bronchitis, backache, cramps, colds and flu, jaundice, kidneys, liver, multiple sclerosis (MS), nerves, sense of smell, spleen, stomach, wind pains, bile ducts, and mineral balance.
Emotional/spiritual: aids diagnosis of illness. Helps with loneliness and keeping your spirits up. Good for yin/yang balance, the aura, achieving goals, dowsing, and fasting.

TOURMALINE

Vertically striated prismatic crystals that are found in most colors: green (verdelite), blue (indicolite), pink (elbaite), red (rubellite), yellow (tsilasite), black (schorl), brown (dravite), green or blue with a pink center (watermelon) or vice versa, lime green (often with a white center), and lavender (recently discovered), as well as bi-colors, tri-colors, colorless (achroite), and with distinct bands when sliced and polished (liddicoatite).

Common sources:	Brazil, Pakistan, USA

Reiki symbol: Dai Ko Myo

Chakras: see specific tourmaline varieties

Reiki tip: wear tourmaline to protect you from your client's energy during treatments (see Chapter 3).

HEALING QUALITIES

Physical: aids digestion. Good for the lymphatic system, bladder, detoxing, and managing low blood pressure.
Emotional/spiritual: calming and brings balance. Helps you embrace new challenges and digest ideas. Good for all mental health and healing. Helps with fear, breakdowns, removing blockages, a restless mind, bipolar disorder, schizophrenia, stubbornness, a victim mentality, anxiety, and a troubled mind. Combats negativity and worrying too much what others think. Offers protection on all levels, from simple accidents to psychic attack and evil curses! Enhances negotiation skills, inspiration, self-confidence, and creativity. Good for yin/yang balance, awareness, all psychic abilities, healing ability, connection, left/right brain balance, working in groups, connecting with your inner-self, happiness, and laughter therapy. Tourmaline wand crystals (long, thin crystals) focus energy to areas where it is most needed and are excellent for affirmations and aura healing.

FLUORITE

Cubic, octahedral, and rhombododecahedral crystals and masses. Colors include purple, clear, blue, green, yellow, brown, pink, red, black, and rainbow fluorite (which may include green, purple, blue and clear/colorless bands in the same specimen).

Common alternative name: fluor spar

Common sources: China, Mexico, Republic of South Africa, UK, USA, worldwide

Reiki symbol: Cho Ku Rei

Chakra: brow

Reiki tip: if you're working at a computer for any length of time, keep some fluorite nearby to counteract the tiring effects of looking at the screen.

HEALING QUALITIES

Physical: good for promoting weight gain, blood vessels, backache and lumbago, detoxing, colds, flu, virulent infections, herpes, ulcers, and the early stages of cancer, as well as the health of bones, the spleen, and teeth.

Emotional/spiritual: helps with eating disorders (such as anorexia and bulimia), overexcitement, and stress, because it focuses the mind, allowing it to work effectively in stressful situations, and brings order out of chaos. Good for making decisions, concentration, relationships, working in groups, and meditation.

CALCITE

Occurs as masses, stalactites, scalenohedral, and rhombohedral crystals. Common colors include green, blue, yellow, golden, orange, clear (Iceland spa), white, brown, pink, red, black, and gray.

Common sources: worldwide

Reiki symbol: Sei He Ki

Chakras: see specific calcite varieties

Reiki tip: calcite helps you to go through fear and emerge in a brighter place.

HEALING QUALITIES

Physical: good for the health of the kidneys, pancreas, spleen, and bones, especially calcium deficiency.

Emotional/spiritual: a calming, feel-better stone. Every variety of calcite is calming in different ways (for example, green calcite calms the emotions and nerves, whereas blue calcite calms the mind). Helps with overenthusiasm, fear, and stress. Balances emotions and yin/yang energy. Good for astral travel, channeling, teaching and studying (especially art and science), and seeing the bigger picture.

BLUE

LAPIS LAZULI

Occurs as massive rock, which almost always includes lazurite, calcite, and pyrite, and cubic and dodecahedral crystals.

Common sources: Afghanistan, Chile

Reiki symbol: Cho Ku Rei

Chakra: brow

Reiki tip: boosts intuition and intuitive healing skills.

HEALING QUALITIES

Physical: good for the bones, bone marrow, backache, throat, thymus, thyroid, vitality, and immune system. Helps with detoxing, vertigo, dizziness, hearing loss, and the health of the Eustachian tube.

Emotional/spiritual: a feel-better stone bringing appreciation and happiness into your life. Encourages creative expression, relaxation, wisdom, all psychic abilities, natural gifts and skills, and dreams. Helps with depression, insomnia, mental endurance, being disorganized, a yin/yang balance, and relationships.

AQUA AURA

A quartz crystal that is bonded with gold, creating beautiful, mostly clear blue crystals and clusters.

Common source: USA (from Arkansas or Brazilian quartz), at the time of writing there is relatively new production in China, so far, the quality is significantly lower

Reiki symbol: Sei He Ki

Chakras: brow, throat

Reiki tip: work with this crystal for any type of trauma; it has an almost instant response when needed.

HEALING QUALITIES

Physical: good for the ear, nose, and throat. Improves the senses—feeling, hearing, sight, smell, and taste.

Emotional/spiritual: a feel-better stone that helps with shock, trauma, negativity, depression, sadness, loss, and grief. Heals and strengthens the aura. Good for communication, protection, and all psychic abilities.

BLUE LACE AGATE

A pale blue and white banded variety of agate.

Common source: Republic of South Africa

Reiki symbol: Sei He Ki

Chakra: throat

Reiki tip: work with blue lace agate for attunements (see page 14).

HEALING QUALITIES

Physical: good for the eyesight, speech (especially a stammer), pancreas, and nails. Helps with arthritis, fluid retention, trapped nerves, skin growths, and broken bones and fractures. Soothes tired eyes (as an elixir).

Emotional/spiritual: very gentle and calming, bringing peace to most situations, as well as balance and emotional stability. Raises your spiritual level and improves communication on all levels, especially of spiritual ideas.

AQUAMARINE

A blue/green variety of beryl that forms hexagonal prismatic crystals, usually with flat terminations.

Common sources: Afghanistan, Brazil, Namibia, Pakistan, USA

Reiki symbol: Cho Ku Rei

Chakra: throat

Reiki tip: helps things flow in your life, allowing events to unfold.

HEALING QUALITIES

Physical: good for the kidneys, lymphatic system, blood, brain, eyes, and teeth. Helps all conditions related to bodily fluids, such as water retention, swelling, detoxing, and swollen glands. Improves eyesight. Cooling in hot climates.

Emotional/spiritual: provides protection for travelers. Calming and good for communication, courage, intellect, study, and learning. Very gently washes away energy blocks in chakras. Enhances spiritual awareness and development. Centering and helps with meditation. Helps you accept the truth about yourself and connect to your inner-self and higher-self. Encourages compassion, responsibility for your own actions, and tolerance, combating a judgmental attitude.

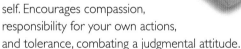

BLUE CALCITE

Found as blue/pale blue masses.

Common source: Mexico

Reiki symbol: Sei He Ki

Chakra: throat

Reiki tip: good for performing Crystal Reiki Healing treatments on children.

HEALING QUALITIES

Physical: good for the pharynx and voice, so helps with throat infections and laryngitis.

Emotional/spiritual: mentally and spiritually calming. Good for ADHD, expression, and communication.

AZURITE

Found as masses, nodules, and, rarely, tabular and prismatic crystals, in azure or paler blues.

Common alternative name: blue malachite

Common sources: China, Morocco, USA

Reiki symbol: Sei He Ki

Chakras: throat, brow

Reiki tip: promotes an empathic connection with your clients.

HEALING QUALITIES

Physical: increases blood strength. Good for the nervous system and arthritis.

Emotional/spiritual: known as the "stone of heaven," it enhances creativity and psychic abilities. Encourages compassion. Helps you to express feelings, thoughts, and information.

BLUE CHALCEDONY

A light blue variety of chalcedony.

Common source: Republic of South Africa

Reiki symbol: Hon Sha Ze Sho Nen

Chakra: throat

Reiki tip: excellent for dealing with childhood issues.

HEALING QUALITIES

Physical: good for the throat, mouth, gums, and teeth.
Emotional/spiritual: helps with addictions (such as alcoholism) and changing unhealthy behavior patterns. Encourages communication and emotional expression.

CELESTITE

Tabular orthorhombic crystals that occur as nodules and masses in shades of blue, but also in white, yellow, orange, red, and reddish-brown.

Common source: Madagascar

Reiki symbol: Dai Ko Myo

Chakras: brow, crown

Reiki tip: connects you to your Reiki guides.

HEALING QUALITIES

Physical: helps relieve physical pain. Useful in the treatment of eye and hearing problems. Aids detoxing.
Emotional/spiritual: encourages creative expression and natural abilities. Helps you make your dreams come true. Good for relaxation, managing stress and worries, speech, clear thought, dreams, dream recall, dealing with nightmares and night terrors, yin/yang balance and astral travel. Very helpful in mental activities with complex ideas. A crystal linked very strongly to angels. Promotes love with respect, music, art, and meditation. Helps relieve despair and mental disorders.

DUMORTIERITE

Found as blue masses. Other colors include pink and brown.

Common sources: Brazil, Madagascar

Reiki symbol: Sei He Ki

Chakra: brow

Reiki tip: helps you to understand the cause of dis-ease.

HEALING QUALITIES

Physical: good for tendons and ligaments, so helps with tendonitis and tennis elbow.
Emotional/spiritual: calms excitability. Combats stubbornness. Encourages quiet confidence (making it easier for you to speak your mind), stamina, patience, expression, communication, and insight.

SAPPHIRE

A gem variety of corundum found in every color except red (which is ruby)—blue, yellow (oriental topaz), green (oriental emerald), black, purple/violet (oriental amethyst), pink, and white.

Common sources: India, Madagascar, Sri Lanka, Thailand

Reiki symbol: Dai Ko Myo

Chakra: brow

Reiki tip: helps with attunements.

HEALING QUALITIES

Physical: helps all glands function correctly and good for glandular fever. Helps with infection, nausea, backache, boils, and blood clotting. Good for the heart, hormones, and stomach. Has astringent properties.

Emotional/spiritual: helps you fulfil your ambitions, dreams, and goals. Brings emotional balance, wisdom, spiritual connection, and connection to your spirit guides. Enhances intuition. Helps with controlling desire, aging, depression, narrow-mindedness, and unhappiness. Brings fun, happiness, and joy into your life. Helps you see the beauty in everything,

TANZANITE

A variety of zoisite that forms masses and stunning blue prismatic striated crystals. Other colors include yellow, gray/blue, and purple.

Common source: Tanzania

Reiki symbol: Dai Ko Myo

Chakras: throat, brow, crown

Reiki tip: boosts the flow of Reiki and helps Reiki "speak" to you.

HEALING QUALITIES

Physical: good for the eyes and skin and aides a healthy complexion. Helps with fatigue.

Emotional/spiritual: encourages communication and connection to spirit guides. Helps you understand the language of the Stone People (crystals). Good for all psychic abilities, meditation, visualization, magic, and emotional and mental exhaustion.

SODALITE

Found as blue or blue and white masses, nodules, and, rarely, dodecahedral and hexagonal prismatic crystals. Other colors include gray, green, yellow, white, red, and clear.

Common source: Brazil

Reiki symbol: Sei He Ki

Chakra: brow

Reiki tip: great for integrating groups of people who are new to each other in Reiki classes.

HEALING QUALITIES

Physical: good for high blood pressure, physical balance, the lymphatic system, diabetes, metabolism, healthy development of babies, and calcium deficiency.

Emotional/spiritual: calming. Helps with fear, insomnia, mental health and healing, mental unrest, oversensitivity, autism, Asperger's syndrome, aging, confusion, and feelings of inadequacy. Builds self-esteem. Encourages creative expression and endurance. Enhances perception. Helps you communicate feelings and ideas.

TURQUOISE

Occurs as blue, green, or blue/green masses and crusts.

Common sources: China, Myanmar, Tibet, USA

Reiki symbol: Dai Ko Myo

Chakra: throat

Reiki tip: gives protection to travelers—bearing in mind that a journey can be a trip around the world or a walk to the convenience store.

HEALING QUALITIES

Physical: the go-to crystal for all allergic reactions (such as hayfever and skin rashes). A general multipurpose healer for the body, it helps with general malaise, arthritis, rheumatism, backache, common cold, flu, detoxing, circulation, absorption of nutrients, tissue regeneration, promotes weight gain, wind pains, travel sickness, air, sea and motion sickness, cataracts, wounds, post-operative recovery, headaches, and whiplash. Good for the lungs, so helps asthma, bronchitis, and breathing. Enhances health of the throat and muscles. As an elixir it helps treat stress-related skin disorders (see Reiki water, page 50). Alleviates reactions to radiation (such as skin rashes and nausea) and side effects of chemotherapy, radiotherapy, and similar types of medication. Helps with food intolerances.

Emotional/spiritual: encourages communication, public speaking, creative expression, friendship, both physical and spiritual love, compassion, romance, travel, spirituality, peace of mind, all psychic abilities, wisdom, and seeing the beauty in everything. Brings courage, emotional balance, protection of property and from accidents, and mental and spiritual clarity to see your own path and walk your walk. Grounding during peak experiences in meditation. Assists spirit contact, astral travel, yin/yang balance, and writing. Counteracts a suspicious mind and negativity.

VIOLET

CHAROITE

Found as masses, sometimes with inclusions of white quartz and black manganese.

Common source: Russia

Reiki symbol: Raku

Chakra: crown

Reiki tip: charoite helps to keep you in the moment.

HEALING QUALITIES

Physical: good for the eyes, heart, headaches, general aches and pains, liver damage (sclerosis of the liver), pancreatic damage, pulse rate, and detoxing (as an elixir).

Emotional/spiritual: brings your spiritual experiences into your physical world. Breaks cycles and unhelpful behavior patterns set in the past. Assists analysis so helps you work out answers and meaning, and also meditation, clairvoyance, intuition, moving forward, and releasing old relationships. Good for autism and Asperger's syndrome, Improves attention span and helps ADHD. Helps you see opportunities.

VIOLET FLAME OPAL

A variety of common opal (displays no fire) which is white and violet, ranging from purple to lilac and blue.

Common alternative names: violet ray opal, purple ray opal, Mexican purple opal

Common source: Mexico

Reiki symbol: Hon Sha Ze Sho Nen

Chakra: crown

Reiki tip: heals your aura and protects your energy by acting as a protective shield, which allows you to create effective personal boundaries. This is very useful for Crystal Reiki Healers and all therapists.

HEALING QUALITIES

Physical: good for fertility, the digestive system, absorption of nutrients, immune system, temperature control, fever, hypothermia, hair loss, eyes, eyesight, the effects of EMF, pancreas, and diabetes. Enhances the senses—hearing, sight, smell, taste, and touch.

Emotional/spiritual: eases trauma, shock, and changes that could be traumatic. Enhances mediumship and connection to spirit, angels, spirit guides and helpers, and totem animals. Assists gentle release of painful emotions and hurts, such as anger and fear, and transforms them into positive feelings and actions, such as love and compassion. Encourages awareness, visions, and spiritual strength. Helps you digest new ideas and concepts.

LEPIDOLITE

Usually found as lavender (pink to purple) masses and layered plates ("books"), but sometimes also as short prismatic and tabular crystals. Other colors include yellow, gray, colorless, and white.

Common source: Brazil

Reiki symbol: Hon Sha Ze Sho Nen

Chakras: heart, brow

Reiki tip: good for learning new skills.

HEALING QUALITIES

Physical: eases the birth process. Good for digestion, tendonitis, cramps, constipation, nerves, and an erratic heartbeat. Reduces wrinkles (as an elixir).

Emotional/spiritual: helpful in the treatment of all addictions and those with addictive personalities. Helps with studying, stress and related conditions, depression, changes and transition (including death/dying), and re-birth. Enhances awareness and astral travel. Counteracts distrust. Calming.

Other: good for abundant crops.

SUGILITE

Found as violet masses, often with inclusions, and, rarely, tiny crystals.

Common alternative names: lavulite, royal lavulite, royal azel

Common source: Republic of South Africa

Reiki symbol: Dai Ko Myo

Chakra: crown

Reiki tip: sugilite helps most conditions, so is a good crystal to have in your collection.

HEALING QUALITIES

Physical: helps you to see and understand the mind-body link in disease, so is helpful in the treatment of most illnesses. Good for the adrenal, pineal, and pituitary glands, as well as headaches, epilepsy, and chronic physical discomfort and pain.

Emotional/spiritual: brings mental balance, confidence, and courage. Good for Indigo Children, autism and Asperger's syndrome, children with learning difficulties, and dyslexia. Encourages spiritual love, spirit contact, finding your life path, creativity and forgiveness. Helps with eccentricity—it doesn't "cure" it, but helps you be who you are. Counteracts hostility, anger, jealousy, prejudice, and despair.

SUPER SEVEN

A type of quartz with inclusions that appears primarily purple in color, but is comprised of seven different minerals: amethyst, cacoxenite, goethite, lepidocrocite, quartz, rutile, and smoky quartz. Due to the included minerals, it may have areas that appear brown, red, white, black, or colorless. Smaller pieces exhibit all the healing qualities, even if all seven different minerals are not present in the specimen—the original mass gives super seven its wonderful healing potential.

Common alternative names: Super 7, Sacred Seven, Melody Stone (after the American crystal healer and author Melody)

Only source: Espirito Santo (Brazil)

Reiki symbol: Dai Ko Myo

Chakras: all

Reiki tip: helps to speed clients (and you) through any karmic healing that's needed.

HEALING QUALITIES

Physical: good for the nervous system.
Emotional/spiritual: boosts the aura and helps you to see auras. Promotes a connection to spirit. Helps you understand the language of the Stone People. Enhances psychic awareness. Encourages truth, advancement, and fulfilment of dreams, goals, and ideals, peace, harmony, and love. Connected to karma, reincarnation, and past lives. Good for telepathy, clairaudience, clairvoyance, creativity, and Earth healing.

SPIRIT QUARTZ

Found as violet (amethyst) or white (quartz) clusters of crystals with profuse barnacle crystal growth, sometimes with orange/brown iron inclusions or surface staining.

Common source: Republic of South Africa

Reiki symbol: Sei He Ki

Chakra: crown

Reiki tip: helps you see and release your dark side.

HEALING QUALITIES

Physical: good for fertility and skin allergies (as an elixir). Helps all functions and conditions related to fluids (such as blood, lymph, swelling, fluid retention, and detoxing).
Emotional/spiritual: generates a sense of belonging so helps loneliness and is good for team building in groups, work environments, and sports. Helps with grief, obsessive behavior and OCD, rebirthing, and fear of success. Releases and revitalizes emotions. Enhances meditation, astral travel, dreams, connection to past experiences, past lives, and the inner/higher-self, ESP, and flow. Encourages abundance, patience, and self-esteem. Brings protection.

WHITE/CLEAR

HERKIMER DIAMOND

A clear, stubby, double-terminated quartz crystal.

Only source: Herkimer County (New York State, USA). Other "diamond-style" quartz crystals are available from locations such as Pakistan, Mexico, and Romania, but these are not the same.

Reiki symbol: Dai Ko Myo

Chakra: crown

Reiki tip: an excellent crystal to have under the attunement chair, as it helps the Master connect to the student's energy (see page 14).

HEALING QUALITIES

Physical: good for detoxing, metabolism, and repair of damaged genetic material, genes, and chromosomes. and cellular genetic material. Alleviates the effects of radiation, as well as side effects of chemotherapy and radiotherapy. **Emotional/spiritual:** promotes being in the moment. Relieves stress and fear. Encourages spontaneity, relaxation, and new beginnings. Good for all psychic abilities and memory. Enhances connection to energies, people, places, deities, ceremony, crystals, Reiki, and just about anything else.

APOPHYLLITE

Cubic and pyramidal crystals, druses, and masses. Commonly white or colorless, or, rarely, green.

Common source: India

Reiki symbol: Dai Ko Myo

Chakras: brow, crown

Reiki tip: helps to continue a meditative state.

HEALING QUALITIES

Physical: good for eyesight, tissue repair, and skin rejuvenation. Helps maintain youthful appearance. **Emotional/spiritual:** helps create and maintain your connection to spirit. Promotes truth, brain power, and problem solving. Good for astral travel, reflection and connecting with nner-self, scrying, and clairvoyance. **Other:** apophyllite pyramids can help preserve food.

DANBURITE

Clear/white prismatic striated crystals. Other colors include pink, yellow, and lilac.

Common sources: Mexico, USA

Reiki symbol: Sei He Ki

Chakra: crown

Reiki tip: can help a new class or group to bond.

HEALING QUALITIES

Physical: eases muscle stiffness. Good for the gall bladder, liver, detoxing, and helps weight gain. **Emotional/spiritual:** socialization—helps you get back into the world after an absence, such as grief, breakdown, drug problems, or hospitalization. Good for groups and teams. Helps with postoperative depression.

HOWLITE

Generally found as white or off-white nodules and masses. Often dyed and used to imitate turquoise—turquoise blue howlite is very common.

Common source: USA

Reiki symbol: Cho Ku Rei

Chakra: crown

Reiki tip: good for clients who are recovering from surgery.

HEALING QUALITIES

Physical: boosts the immune system. Eases physical pain. Good for the teeth and bones.

Emotional/spiritual: promotes action—it's like it gives you a kick to get you going! Encourages calm communication, being discerning, and emotional expression. Boosts memory. Good for studying. Helps you focus on goals. Helps with selfishness, stress, anger, boisterousness, and vulgarity.

MOONSTONE

A variety of feldspar that exhibits chatoyancy. Colors include white, cream, yellow, brown, blue, green (parrot moonstone), and rainbow, which is white with a blue color flash.

Common source: India

Reiki symbol: Dai Ko Myo

Chakra: sacral

Reiki tip: promotes empathy, which is a useful quality for any healer.

HEALING QUALITIES

Physical: helps with fertility, pregnancy, childbirth, female hormones, menstrual cycle and menstruation, period pains and PMS, menopause, circulation, constipation,

water retention, swelling, and insect bites. Good for anaphylactic shock once the emergency is dealt with. Good for the pituitary gland, eyes, skin (as a topical elixir), hair (as a topical elixir), and a youthful appearance.

Emotional/spiritual: helps to create a happy home. Calming and soothing. Helps with emotions generally, control, balance, oversensitivity, sexuality, and passion. Releases energy blocks. Promotes a caring attitude, compassion, kindness, nurture, wisdom, and peace of mind. Helps you connect to your inner self. Breaks cycles and repeated patterns. Helps manage change, new beginnings, and endings. Counteracts pessimism. Enhances intuition, insight, creativity, confidence, and composure. Gives protection to travelers. Brings good luck.

SNOW QUARTZ

Quartz that occurs as white masses.

Common alternative names: quartzite, milky quartz, female quartz

Common sources: worldwide (especially India and USA)

Reiki symbol: Dai Ko Myo

Chakra: crown

Reiki tip: produces a sense of purity so is good for Reiki Masters to carry or wear during attunements.

HEALING QUALITIES

Physical: good for the brain, spine, and nerves. Helps with Alzheimer's disease and dementia.

Emotional/spiritual: clears the mind of confusing thoughts and worry, bringing clarity and wisdom. Removes mental blockages. Boosts memory. Counteracts negativity. Good for study and exam revision.

TOURMALINATED QUARTZ

Quartz crystals and masses with black tourmaline crystal rods growing through them.

Common alternative name: tourmaline in quartz

Common source: Brazil

Reiki symbol: Sei He Ki

Chakras: all

Reiki tip: helps to change unhelpful behavior patterns.

HEALING QUALITIES

Physical: good for the nervous system.

Emotional/spiritual: helps to illuminate the path ahead of you, so particularly good for small business owners. Helps you let go of the past and deal with childhood experiences. Helps with depression, fear, tension, and nervous exhaustion. Good for problem solving, calculating, and mathematics, so good for those with acalculia (loss of the ability to perform calculations) and accountants.

SELENITE

A crystallized form of gypsum that is usually clear or white.

Common sources: Mexico, Morocco (for satin spa variety), USA

Reiki symbol: Dai Ko Myo

Chakra: crown

Reiki tip: good for all types of cycles—it enhances the helpful ones and breaks the troublesome ones.

HEALING QUALITIES

Physical: good for longevity and skin elasticity, wrinkles, and age spots, giving a youthful appearance. Helps skin conditions, such as acne, eczema, psoriasis, and skin sensitivity. Helps with epilepsy, hair loss, loss of fertility, light sensitivity, effects of leakage from mercury amalgam fillings, and conditions associated with free radicals, including, cancer and tumors. Good for the spine and menstrual cycle.

Emotional/spiritual: good for sex drive. Helps you deal with abuse, stress, and worry. Alleviates stress-related skin conditions. Strongly linked with the moon (selenite is named after Selene, goddess of the moon).

GODDESS STONE

A white, gray, and brown mineraloid opal, technically known as menilite. Forms natural bulbous shapes that resemble prehistoric goddess figures.

Common alternative names: menilite, fairy stone, menalite (common misspelling)

Common sources: France, Morocco

Reiki symbol: Dai Ko Myo

Chakra: crown

Reiki tip: promotes femininity and boosts connection to the sacred feminine.

HEALING QUALITIES

Physical: good for fertility and the female reproductive system.

Emotional/spiritual: enhances your connection to the Goddess and the energies of the moon and Gaia (Mother Earth). Conveys love, nurture, comfort, protection, safety, and mystery. Brings out your hidden talents. Gives inner strength and confidence, dispelling fear and allowing sexuality to come to the fore. Brings manifestation, abundance, and new beginnings. Helps develop intuition, divination, and other psychic skills.

BLACK

BLACK OBSIDIAN
Black volcanic glass.

Common sources: Mexico, USA

Reiki symbol: Raku

Chakra: base

Reiki tip: acts as a mirror of the soul—enables you to take a long, deep, hard look at yourself and then smile.

HEALING QUALITIES

Physical: good for digestion, the colon, gastroenteritis, IBS, Crohn's disease, wind pains, nausea, diarrhea, and constipation.

Emotional/spiritual: helps to release subconscious blockages, allowing you to let go of things you didn't even realize affected you. Good for grounding, protection, survival instinct, creativity, intuition, scrying, integrating spirituality into your everyday life, wisdom, seeing your dark side, and learning. Enhances male qualities, energies, and sexuality. Supports shamanic healing. Helps you recognize the cause of dis-ease, connect to your roots and past experiences, and break self-defeating patterns.

BLACK TOURMALINE
Black, vertically striated prismatic crystals.

Common alternative names: schorl, afrisite

Common sources: Brazil, India, Pakistan

Reiki symbol: Cho Ku Rei

Chakra: base

Reiki tip: wear black tourmaline when giving treatments to protect yourself from picking up the energy that your clients release.

HEALING QUALITIES

Physical: good for vitality, arthritis, the heart, and adrenal glands. Alleviates the effects of radiation, including the side-effects from chemotherapy and radiotherapy.

Emotional/spiritual: protects you from all types and sources of negativity. Counteracts a victim mentality. Encourages emotional stability, intellect, practicality, creativity, and connection to the Earth. A feel-better stone that eases anxiety and embarrassment. Helps with clumsiness and dyslexia.

JET
The fossilized remains of trees. It is always much lighter in weight than you would expect for its size.

Common sources: Canada, China, Germany, Russia (specifically Siberia), Spain, Turkey, UK (jet from Whitby is renowned as the premium grade), USA

Reiki symbol: Sei He Ki

Chakra: base

Reiki tip: helps clients to release grief.

HEALING QUALITIES

Physical: protects against illnesses. Helps with migraines, swollen glands, stomachache, digestion, epilepsy, and common colds.

Emotional/spiritual: protects against violence, and together with red jasper guards against witchcraft.

Helps deal with loss, the end of a long-term relationship, letting go, depression, and fear. Enhances sexual energy and a yin/yang balance. Brings wealth. Grounding and brings energy with calmness.

MERLINITE

Black and white moss opal.

Common alternative names: opalite (please note that opalite is also a trade name for a manmade glass with rainbow colors but it is not the same crystal)

Common sources: India, Turkey, USA

Reiki symbol: Raku

Chakra: brow

Reiki tip: removes energy blocks and promotes flow, allowing you to move forward in life.

HEALING QUALITIES

Physical: enhances sexual energy, survival instincts, and physical reserves of energy. Improves metabolism.

Emotional/spiritual: helps you to seize the moment. Enhances all psychic abilities. Lets you see both sides of an argument. Helps you access akashic records. Calming. Balances yin/yang. Encourages magic and optimism.

APACHE TEAR

Small translucent nodules of obsidian that are black or brown.

Common source: USA

Reiki symbol: Sei He Ki

Chakra: base

Reiki tip: helps release suppressed tears and emotions.

HEALING QUALITIES

Physical: good for the knees, vitamin C and D deficiencies, muscle spasms, and detoxing. Traditional snakebite remedy: held to the wound but carried or worn 24/7 to promote healing.

Emotional/spiritual: frees you from self-limiting beliefs. Helps with changing behavior, emotional balance, grief, negativity, and moving on from past lives. Promotes change and moving forward in life. Encourages forgiveness and spontaneity.

SNOWFLAKE OBSIDIAN

Black obsidian with inclusions of white phenocryst that form "snowflake" patterns.

Common source: USA

Reiki symbol: Raku

Chakra: base

Reiki tip: helps to release anger.

HEALING QUALITIES

Physical: good for stomach and sinuses, because it unblocks the meridian linking these two areas, as well as the veins, bones, eyesight, eyes (as an elixir), skin (as an elixir). Helps with acalculia and detoxing.

Emotional/spiritual: brings peace of mind. Helps you let go of resentment. Helps with unhelpful behavior patterns and loneliness. Enhances meditation and purity (in all senses).

SHUNGITE

Opaque and lustrous black, charcoal-colored or brown non-crystalline mineral. Includes up to 98% carbon.

Common alternative names: fullerite, fullerene, bucky balls, Buckminsterfullerene, black ocher (no relationship to red and yellow ocher)

Common sources: top-quality shungite is only found in the Zazhoginskoye deposit near Lake Onega in the Shunga region of Karelia, northwest Russia; lower-quality shungite is available from Austria, Democratic Republic of Congo, India, and Kazakhstan

Reiki symbol: Dai Ko Myo

Chakras: all

Reiki tip: purifies water—place shungite stones in your Reiki water (see page 50).

HEALING QUALITIES

Physical: good for detoxing (as an elixir). Helps recovery from illness, disease, injury, and surgery. Promotes growth, tissue repair, and the healthy development of children. Good for allergic skin reactions and chronic pain relief.

Emotional/spiritual: can help stress-related allergies. Cleanses and purifies mind, body, and spirit. Protects you from EMF and geopathic stress. Brings balance. Aids emotional and spiritual recovery from illness. Good for stress and emotional pain relief. Cleanses your emotions—it helps you to let go of anything that is holding you back.

TEKTITE

Meteoritic glass that has been created by the immense heat of a meteorite impact with the earth. The heat is so intense that both the meteorite and the Earth's surface melt, and tektite is formed as this mixture of space material and Earth cool together. Usually black or brown in color; also, rarely, yellow (Libyan glass) and green (moldavite).

Common sources: China, Thailand

Reiki symbol: Hon Sha Ze Sho Nen

Chakra: crown

Reiki tip: helpful for Reiki Masters practicing psychic surgery.

HEALING QUALITIES

Physical: good for fertility, fever, and circulation.
Emotional/spiritual: emotionally bridges the physical distance between friends, relatives, and lovers, so good for homesickness. Encourages yin/yang balance and abundance. Good for reasoning, telepathy, meditation (getting started and reaching and maintaining peak experience), and contact with other worlds.

GRAY

HEMATITE

Occurs as masses, botryoidal forms, rosettes, layered "plates", and tabular and rhombohedral crystals. Black and brick red/brown in color, or typically metallic gray/silver when polished.

Common sources: worldwide (especially Morocco and UK)

Reiki symbol: Raku

Chakra: base

Reiki tip: good for grounding; hold a couple of hematite stones if you are feeling a little spacy after giving a treatment, and keep them in your therapy room for your clients in case they feel floaty after a treatment and need to drive home.

HEALING QUALITIES

Physical: good for all blood conditions, including anemia and blood clots, and the spleen. Helps with cramps, MS, backache, airsickness, travel sickness, jet lag, dexterity, broken bones, and fractures. Cools body temperature so helps fever (as an elixir) and sunburn (as a topical elixir). Good for vertebrae (place one stone at the base of the spine and one stone at the top).

Emotional/spiritual: brings courage and strength. Increases personal magnetism. Helps with stress, insomnia, mental processes, thoughts, memory, numbers/maths, acalculia, yin/yang balance, and negativity. Attracts love. Good for meditation.

GRAY BANDED AGATE

A gray and white banded or patterned variety of agate that occurs as masses.

Common source: Botswana

Reiki symbol: Cho Ku Rei

Chakra: sacral

Reiki tip: stores energy and releases it as a boost to your physical energy when you need it.

HEALING QUALITIES

Physical: eases fatigue, general malaise, and ME. Good for digestion, the bowel, and IBS.

Emotional/spiritual: gives you confidence and your mojo back. Offers protection.

PYRITE

Occurs as cubic and dodecahedral crystals, occasionally flattened (pyrite suns) and masses. It becomes more golden with oxidation and may replace many minerals, so can be found in many other formations and in combination with other minerals.

Common alternative names: iron pyrites, fool's gold; marcasite is chemically the same but has a different crystalline structure

Common sources: Peru, Spain, UK, USA

Reiki symbol: Cho Ku Rei

Chakras: all, but especially solar plexus

Reiki tip: it's like sparks of energy—physical, emotional, mental, and spiritual.

HEALING QUALITIES

Physical: good for circulation, digestion, varicose veins, the brain, snoring, pollution, bones, formation of cells, radiation sickness and side effects of chemotherapy and radiotherapy, lungs, asthma, bronchitis, pleurisy, infection, fever, and inflammation.

Emotional/spiritual: encourages leadership, inspiration, ideas, plans, and goals. Counteracts negativity. Good for memory, thought processes, and protection. Helps if you are accident prone.

Other: place pyrite on your windowsills or by doors or shared walls in apartments or townhouses/terraced housing to quieten noisy neighbors.

STIBNITE

Found as columns, blades, needle-like and prismatic crystals with obvious vertical striations, and masses.

Common sources: China, Uzbekistan

Reiki symbol: Dai Ko Myo

Chakra: crown

Reiki tip: assists Reiki Masters to clearly communicate information to students.

HEALING QUALITIES

Physical: improves reactions, speed, and endurance. Good for muscles, nerves, stiffness, the stomach, and esophagus.

Emotional/spiritual: helps you to find direction and make choices and decisions. Good for teaching and meditation, as it helps to stop distractions and keep your focus. Protects you from "evil spirits." Good for managing money, clingy relationships, and loyalty in relationships. Enhances attractiveness. Connects with the wolf (teacher and path finder), and helps you discover your totem animals.

NO ELIXIR

BROWN

PETRIFIED WOOD

Formed from fossilized trees in which the organic material has been replaced by one or more minerals—usually agate, chalcedony, and quartz, but many other types can be present. May be brown, but can be any wood-like color, or the colors of agate, chalcedony, and opal.

Common sources: worldwide (especially Madagascar and USA)

Reiki symbol: Hon Sha Ze Sho Nen

Chakra: base

Reiki tip: helps you connect to past lives, recall events, and heal.

HEALING QUALITIES

Physical: good for arthritis, allergies, hayfever, infection, longevity, effects of pollution, bones, and broken bones and fractures.

Emotional/spiritual: brings stability to wobbling emotions and mental balance. Soothing and grounding. Helps with stress and childhood issues.

CRAZY LACE AGATE

A variety of agate with "crazy" patterns—bands and wavy lines of brown, cream, and red.

Common alternative name: Mexican lace agate

Common source: Mexico

Reiki symbol: Cho Ku Rei

Chakra: heart

Reiki tip: carry this whenever you do something new.

HEALING QUALITIES

Physical: good for vitality, the heart, skin (as an elixir), speech, and senses—hearing, sight, smell, taste, and touch.

Emotional/spiritual: the go-to crystal for confidence, encouraging self-assurance, courage, and self-esteem. Helps with fear, balance, change, and new beginnings.

FULGURITE

A naturally fused quartz with various impurities, giving the shades of color from brown to gray. Formed by lightning strikes in deserts.

Common alternative names: petrified lightning, lechatelierite (a variety of fulgurite)

Common source: Libya

Reiki symbol: Raku

Chakra: brow

Reiki tip: especially helpful for dowsing (see page 46).

HEALING QUALITIES

Physical: good for the ears, nose, throat, esophagus, intestine, colon, digestion, and senses—hearing, sight, smell, taste, and touch.

Emotional/spiritual: aids communication, concentration, and psychic skills.

BOJI STONE®

A gray/brown spherical or ovoid stone with smooth patterns and/or protrusions. Smooth ones are known as "female," while those with protrusions are "male." Stones are usually worked with in male/female pairs. The stone is mostly comprised of pyrite with some palladium and traces of various other minerals.

Only source: Boji Valley (Colorado, USA); other very similar materials are available and are known as pop rocks, shaman stones, or mochi marbles

Reiki symbol: Raku

Chakras: base if working with one Boji stone or all chakras when working with pairs

Reiki tip: work with these in pairs, one in each hand. They will align the body's energies and balance all the chakras simultaneously. This has the effect of energizing, centering, and grounding the physical body, mind, and spirit together, feeling like a rush of energy through the body.

HEALING QUALITIES

Physical: eases pain. Promotes tissue regeneration and speeds recovery.

Emotional/spiritual: good for bringing new ideas into physical fruition. Removes energy blocks and improves flow of energy. Strengthens the aura. Grounding. Supports communication with animals.

LINGHAM

A brown/cream variety of jasper that is roughly the shape of an American football with rounded ends (or a rugby ball).

Common alternative names:
Shiva Lingham, Narmadeshvara Lingham

Only source: Ganges river and tributaries (India)

Reiki symbol: Dai Ko Myo

Chakras: all

Reiki tip: great for a spiritual detox for you and your clients.

HEALING QUALITIES

Physical: good for body fluids, fluid retention, back pain, the spine, menopause, fertility, and prostate.
Emotional/spiritual: brings deeper understanding. Connects physical and spiritual energy. Enhances connection to your higher self, insight, intuition, relationships, love, and male energy. Helps you reach peak experience in meditation.

SMOKY QUARTZ

A brown or black variety of quartz that is colored by natural radiation from the earth. This process can be duplicated in laboratories quite effectively, so for many smoky quartz crystals the color is enhanced.

Common alternative names: smokey quartz, cairngorm

Common sources: Brazil, Madagascar, USA

Reiki symbol: Cho Ku Rei

Chakra: base

Reiki tip: speeds up the laws of karma, sending bad energy back to its source!

HEALING QUALITIES

Physical: good for vitality, physical expression, sexual energy, breathing, and posture, as well as the legs, knees, ankles, hands, and feet. Can have a sedative effect. Good for stammers.
Emotional/spiritual: heals the space left by the loss of a person, animal friend, or relationship. Assists dream interpretation. Encourages mental activity, relaxation, letting go of the past, and moving forward in life. Counteracts negativity, anger, depression, despair, and grief. Grounding and good for energy healing modalities, such as channeling energy through your hands for Reiki and spiritual healing. Offers protection, especially during ceremonies. Enhances meditation, male energies, survival instincts, and intuition. Helps you recognize behavior patterns. Curbs an addiction to shopping and overspending.

MUSCOVITE

A variety of mica usually that forms layered "plates," "flowers," "books," scales, and masses, as well as other crystalline forms. Usually brown, but can also occur in green, pink, gray, violet, yellow, red, and white.

Common source: Brazil

Reiki symbol: Sei He Ki

Chakra: heart

Reiki tip: if you worry about "what happens because of my situation to myself and others, family, friends, business partners and anyone else I think relies on me," then stop worrying, get on with your life, and make the world a little better for everyone.

HEALING QUALITIES

Physical: good for allergies, diabetes, hunger, dehydration, and mononucleosis (glandular fever).
Emotional/spiritual: dispels self-doubt, insecurity, and pessimism. Enhances confidence, inner-strength, and emotional expression. Helps with anger, tantrums, excess nervous energy, and speed of thought. Releases painful emotions. Helps you listen to your intuition, move on from past issues, and make major life decisions. Encourages problem solving, connecting to your higher self, shamanic visions, and meditation. Balances sleep patterns and insomnia.

SEPTARIAN

Nodules of clay ironstone into which other minerals—calcite, jasper, dolomite, aragonite, and, occasionally, barite—are deposited through small cracks in the structure. Other minerals may also be present.

Common sources: Australia, Madagascar, USA

Reiki symbol: Raku

Chakra: base

Reiki tip: good for public speaking, so keep some septarian with you if you're teaching or giving a talk or presentation.

HEALING QUALITIES

Physical: increases flexibility. As an elixir, good for the joints, bones, and muscles, and the teeth (use an elixir as a mouthwash). Helps with melanoma.
Emotional/spiritual: enhances your ability to go with the flow. Assists sound therapy and NLP. Good for patience, endurance, tolerance, awareness of the environment, and emotional flexibility.

grids

In this section you will find all the grids used in Chapter 4. You can place your crystals directly onto the page, trace the grid, or photocopy it. The grids are also available to donwload at www.thecrystalhealer.co.uk

GRID FOR PROBLEM-SOLVING

See pages 95–96

GRID FOR HEALING

See page 97

GRID FOR LOVE AND RELATIONSHIPS

See pages 98–99

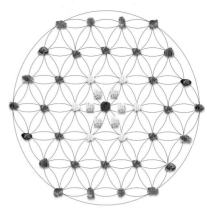

GLOSSARY

ADHD Attention deficit hyperactivity disorder.

Aggregate A mixture of minerals combined in a geological process; resembles a solid rock.

Akashic records A library of spiritual information that exists on another plane.

Asterism An optical effect that results in a star-like appearance.

Astral travel The ability to send a part of the astral/spirit body to travel outside of the physical body (while remaining connected to the physical body).

Attunement The process by which you become connected to Reiki energy so that it can flow through you. There are three levels of Reiki attunement.

Aura The subtle energy field (*qv*) around the body.

Botryoidal Describes bulbous minerals that resemble a bunch of grapes.

Casting stone Stones used in many types of traditional divination, such as runes and witches' stones, and by African and Native American medicine men. There can be many varieties of stone.

CFS Chronic fatigue syndrome, also known as myalgic encephalitis (ME).

Chakra The Sanskrit word for "wheel." Chakras are the energy centers of the body, appearing as spinning balls of energy, like wheels, to people who can see energy

Channeling The communication of messages or information from the spirit world via a medium.

Chatoyancy An optical effect, also known as "cat's eye" found in some polished crystals. Chatoyant crystals bring good luck, happiness, and serenity. They raise intuition and awareness, provide protection, and can help with disorders of the eyes, night vision, and headaches.

Clairaudience The ability to hear psychic information.

Clairsentience The ability to feel psychic energies.

Clairvoyance The ability to see psychic information.

COPD Chronic pulmonary obstructive disease.

Crust The top or outer layer. Crystals occurring as crusts are growing on the surface of a rock or mineral. *See also* Druse.

Cubic Describes a cube-shaped crystal, with six square faces. The three axes are the same length and are at right angles to one another.

Dendrite A mineral that crystallizes in the shape of a tree or branch, or grows through another crystal or rock creating the impression of a tree or branches.

Dis-ease A state of unsoundness on any level (physical, emotional, mental, or spiritual), which may weaken the body's natural defense systems and increase the risk of illness or disease. It relates to underlying causes and not a specific illness or disease.

Distant healing The process of sending healing energy, good thoughts, or prayers to a person who is not physically present. Also known as absent healing or remote healing.

Dodecahedral Describes a crystal having 12 pentagonal (five-sided) faces meeting in threes at 20 vertexes.

Double terminated A crystal with two terminations (*qv*) at opposite ends.

Druse A surface crust of small crystals on a rock of the same or a different mineral.

Earth healing Sending/directing healing energy to the planet.

Elixir Water in which a crystal has been immersed and which is then drunk to treat various conditions. To create an elixir, after cleansing your crystal physically and energetically, place it in a glass of water (ideally distilled or mineral water, but tap water will do), cover, and leave it in the refrigerator overnight. Note that some crystals should never be made into elixirs—these are clearly indicated by 'No elixir' in the Crystal Finder (Chapter 5).

EMF Electromagnetic fields.

ESP Extra-sensory perception.

Feldspar A group of silicate minerals.

Fibrous/fiber A rock made up of roughly parallel fine threads.

Fire A play of color caused by dispersion of light within a crystal, such as that shown by diamonds. Fire opal does not necessarily exhibit fire, but occurs in colors of fire— reds, oranges, yellows. Opal does not display true fire but a play of light caused by the scattering of light by microscopic silica spheres in the opal structure.

Geopathic stress Energy that emanates from the earth and is detrimental to human health. Two sources of this energy may be underground moving water or radiation from cell phone masts. Geopathic stress is linked with a long list of ailments, ranging from headaches to cancer.

Granular A mineral composed of grains. May be formed with rounded, semi-rounded, or angular grains or can be massive (see Mass).

Hexagonal Describes a crystal system having four axes, of which the three horizontal axes are equal in length and cross at 120° angles, and the vertical axis is a different length and at right angles to the others. A hexagonal crystal has eight faces.

IBS Irritable bowel syndrome.

Inclusion A mineral found within the structure of a different mineral.

Indigo children Children with special abilities, often psychic. Most indigo children are now grown adults and are at the forefront of the human consciousness movement..

Iridescence Colors appearing inside a crystal due to either the diffraction or refraction of light within the crystalline structure.

Labradorescence Iridescent flashes of color appearing on the surface of the labradorite crystal.

Karma/karmic process/karmic healing Karma equals action or deed. Also refers to cause and effect and specifically to how the actions of an individual can/will affect his/her future. Karmic healing is about healing karma from past lives or this life so you do not take it with you into the next life, meaning it cannot influence the next life.

Ki The second part of the word "Reiki," Ki is the energy or life force of the universe, believed to flow round the body and to be present in all living things. In other cultures it has different names—for example, chi (China) and prana (India).

Kundalini energy Kundalini is the source of primal energy (chi (*qv*), prana, ki, etc.) and consciousness that we are born with. It comes coiled like a serpent at the base of the spine and can be awakened/raised using various methods such as yoga and crystal healing.

Manifestation The bringing of your dreams, desires, or goals into physical reality.

Mass Matter that has no definable crystalline structure. When the term massive is used, it refers to this rather than to the size of the crystal.

ME Myalgic encephalitis, also known as CFS (chronic fatigue syndrome).

Meridian An energy pathway through the body. Meridians carry ki the same way that veins and arteries carry blood.

Mica Individual member of the mica group of related aluminum silicate minerals that are soft and have perfect basal cleavage (when a mineral has only one cleavage plane), which allows individual members to be "peeled."

Mineraloid A naturally occurring mineral-like substance that does not demonstrate a crystalline structure. Mineraloids have chemical compositions that vary beyond the generally accepted ranges for specific minerals.

MS Multiple sclerosis.

NLP Neuro-linguistic programming.

Nodule A form of mineral that is massive (see Mass) with a rounded outer surface.

OCD Obsessive compulsive disorder.

Octahedral Describes a crystal having eight faces that are all equilateral triangles; resembles two four-sided pyramids joined at the bases.

Orthorhombic Describes a crystal system having three axes of unequal lengths that cross at right angles.

Peak experience A moment of euphoria that can be reached through meditation.

Piezoelectricity The transducer effect that is caused by applying pressure to a crystal. This allows the transmutation of electrical to mechanical energy. This creates a physical vibration which in quartz crystal resonates at a regular and constant frequency. This effect is very stable. So, if you have a quartz watch—and the quartz crystal is pure and cut at the correct angle to its axis—it will be accurate.

Plate A crystal that has grown flattened and often thin.

PMS Premenstrual syndrome. Also known as PMT (premenstrual tension).

Prismatic Describes a crystal having faces that are similar in size and shape and that run parallel to an axis; the ends are rectilinear and similar in size and shape. For example, a triangular prismatic crystal has two triangular ends joined by three rectangular faces, while a hexagonal prismatic crystal has two hexagonal ends connected by six rectangular faces.

Pseudomorph A mineral that replaces another within the original's crystal structure. As a result, the new mineral has the external shape of the departed one.

Psychic abilities These include intuition or gut feelings, channeling (*qv*), clairaudience (*qv*), clairsentience (*qv*), clairvoyance (*qv*), sensing energies, and auras (*qv*), seeing auras, interpreting auras, telepathy, extrasensory perception, and increased insight into divination and tarot card readings.

Psychic attack The intentional energetic assault on one's energy from a distance.

Psychic surgery A technique used to enter the physical body with psychic fingers to remove unhealthy energy.

Pyramidal Describes a crystal in which the base is a polygon (i.e. with at least three straight sides) and the other faces are triangles that meet at a point.

Reiki Master A person who has been attuned to Reiki level 3.

Remote viewing The ability to see places and events at a distance. See *also* Astral travel.

Rhombododecahedral Describes crystals that have 12 equal sides with oblique angles.

Rhombohedral Describes crystals having six faces, each of them a rhombus (which has four equal sides, with opposite sides parallel, and no right angles). A rhombohedron resembles a cube that is skewed to one side.

RNA Ribonucleic acid, genetic material found in cells throughout the body, forms DNA (Deoxyribonucleic acid). Both are essential in coding and expression of genes and essential for most known carbon-based life forms.

Scalenohedral Describes crystals having 12 faces, each of them a scalene triangle (which has three unequal sides).

Scrying Looking into a crystal ball (or obsidian mirror) to see images to predict the future, or to view the past or present.

Shamanic healing An umbrella term covering a multitude of ancient forms of healing, all of which are linked to nature. One of the oldest forms of traditional healing.

Spirit guides The beings or energies of departed souls who impart information, knowledge, and wisdom to help you on your path.

Stalactites Mineral formations descending from the roof of caverns, created as mineral-rich water drips down, facilitating the mineral to deposit over thousands or millions of years.

Striated Describes crystals having parallel grooves or markings along their length.

Tabular Describes crystals that are broad and flat; sometimes shortened to "tabby."

TB Tuberculosis.

Termination The end of the crystal formed by the facets or faces making up the point. Note that a few varieties of crystal have flat terminations, such as some tourmaline and spodumene crystals.

Totem animals Animal spirits or characteristics that help to guide you on your path in life.

Trapezohedral Describes crystals that have trapezium-shaped faces.

index

Page numbers in bold refer to entries in The Crystal Finder (see page 105)

acknowledgments

Every journey has many twists and turns and, as I write this, the 27 years of the Crystal Reiki Healing journey has been quite a trip! So, in historical order, my sincere love and thanks for entering and leaving my journey: Nadine and Lyn, then Bodhini for the kick up the violet ray I needed, and Sarah for all her help and support with this project.

Thanks to Cindy Richards, who continues to be the greatest publisher on the planet, and Carmel Edmonds for her wise editorial input, as well as everyone at CICO Books (with a special mention for Dawn Bates who must be the most patient person on planet publishing) and the people who inspired me to write— my father Cyril, Melody, all my clients and students, and Ian, who knows why.

Rock 'n' Reiki…

courses

Philip Permutt teaches Crystal Healing, Crystal Reiki Healing, Reiki, and meditation in his center in St Albans, UK, and at other venues around the world by arrangement. For details, as well as an online shop, go to www.thecrystalhealer.co.uk. You can also follow Philip on Facebook: www.facebook.com/TheCrystalHealer.

notes

Chapter 1
1. Page 22: Definition taken from lexico.com.
2. Page 32: *The Encyclopedia of Eastern Philosophy and Religion: Buddhism, Taoism, Zen, Hinduism* by Ingrid Fischer-Schreiber, Franz-Karl Ehrhard, Kurt Friedrichs, and Michael S. Diener (Shambhala, 1994)

Chapter 2
1. Page 53: Please be aware that since GDPR came into force in the UK in May 2018, it is your responsibility to ensure that all your client records are secure. Because of this, I advise all my students to keep paper records in a locked filing cabinet and not to store any client information on a computer. You should check any legal requirements in your own country.